Small
Sweaters

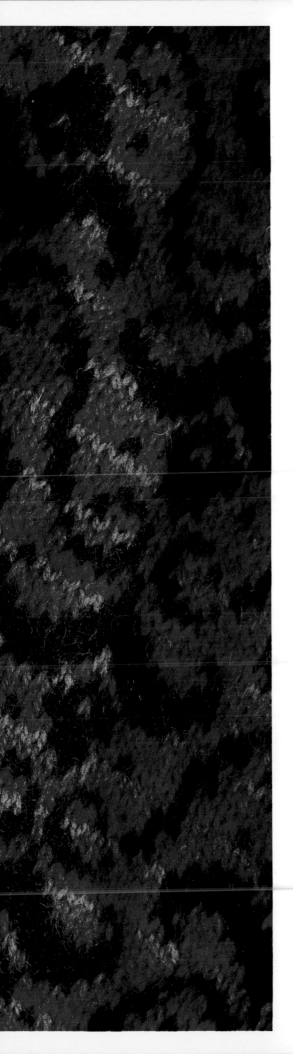

Small Sweaters

Lise Kolstad
Tone Takle

Interweave Press

This book was developed in cooperation with J.W.Cappelens Folag and Rauma Ullvarefabrikk.

Norwegian edition copyright 1995 by J.W. Cappelens Forlag
English language edition copyright 1996 by Interweave Press, Inc.

English translation: Arnhild Hillesland
Photography: Guri Dahl
Stylist: Katrina Vrebalovich
Cover Design: Keith Rosenhagen, Graphic Relations
Production: Marc McCoy Owens

printed in Hong Kong by Sing Cheong

 Interweave Press, Inc.
201 East Fourth Street
Loveland, Colorado 80537-5655
USA

Library of Congress Cataloging-in-Publication Data
Kolstad, Lise.
    [Strikk til barn.   English]
    Small sweaters : colorful knits for kids / by Lise Kolstad and
Tone Takle ; English translation, Arnhild Hillesland ; photography,
Guri Dahl.
        p.   cm.
    Translation of :   Strikk til barn.
    Includes index.
    ISBN 1-883010-22-5
    1. Knitting—Norway—Patterns.   2. Children's clothing.
3. Sweaters.   I. Takle, Tone.   II. Title.
TT825.K6913   1996
746.43'20432—dc20   96-31176
                                                          CIP

First Printing:IWP—10M:996:CC

Contents

Introduction

In this book we present garments whose characteristics reflect those of children—joyful, imaginative, and lively. We include designs for infants to fourteen-year-olds, for novices to experienced knitters. We like to think of this book as a cookbook—just as you might leaf through a cookbook and get the urge to cook, we hope you leaf through this book and get the urge to knit. Use it for inspiration or for a specific "recipe".

Small Sweaters includes patterns for pullovers and cardigans, as well as smaller projects. There are patterns for suits to keep the baby warm, clothes for festive occasions, ski sweaters, coveralls, skirts, tights, and pants. A full chapter is devoted to socks, ski stockings, hats, and mittens. These small projects are ideal for using up leftover bits of yarn.

We hope that *Small Sweaters* will give you many hours of knitting pleasure, and that many children will delight in the warm, lively, handknit outfits that result.

Good luck!
Lise Kolstad and Tone Takle.

Editor's note: This book, translated from Norwegian, was written for knitters who learn to knit by following general patterns and charts. Consequently, the instructions are less detailed than most American patterns. For instance, an instruction may read, "Shape front neck by binding off 31 (33) 35 sts at center front according to the chart." While we may be more accustomed to an instruction that reads, "Shape neck: Following chart, work x stitches, bind off 31 (33) 35 sts, work x stitches", common sense will guide you. If you read through the knitting techniques on pages 9–11 before you begin, you will have the information you need to complete any of the garments in this book.

Knitting Techniques

Shaping a garment is not as difficult as you may think. If you can cast on, increase, and decrease, you have the basics needed to make any kind of garment. These basic techniques are described in this section.

Casting on. The most common cast-on method is the long-tail cast-on. To begin, figure out how long a tail you need to cast on by measuring from the tip of your index finger to your wrist. You'll be able to cast on approximately ten stitches with this length. Measure this length repeatedly, counting by tens until you have enough yarn for the number of stitches you want to cast on. Next, make a slip-knot and place it on a knitting needle. Then put the tail end around your left thumb and the other end around your left index finger. A loop now sits between your thumb and index finger. Hold both tails together with the other fingers on your left hand. Holding the needle in your right hand, bring it to the left side of your left thumb and into the loop that forms around your thumb. Bring the tip of the needle towards the tip of your left index finger, pick up the strand and pull it through the thumb loop, and then slide this loop off your thumb. Repeat until you have the desired number of stitches.

For a more elastic cast-on edge, perhaps for a hat, use the following method: Make a slip-knot and place it on your knitting needle

LONG-TAIL CAST-ON

1. Holding the yarn.

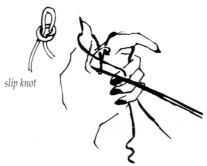

slip knot

2. Make a slip knot around the needle, hold the yarn as shown, and take the needle up through the thumb loop, around the yarn on the left side of the index finger, and back through the thumb loop.

3. Let the loop slip off your left thumb.

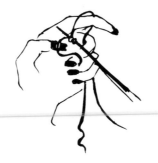

4. Pull up the stitch as you pick up the tail again onto your left thumb.

(you do not need a long tail for this method). Hold this needle in your left hand. With a second needle held in your right hand, knit a new stitch through the loop and put the stitch on the first needle, next to the loop. Then knit a new stitch through the last stitch made, and slip it onto the needle in the same way. Repeat until you have the desired number of stitches.

Increasing. There are many ways to increase stitches. We prefer the increase that makes a stitch out of the horizontal strand that lies between two knitted stitches, called a make-one increase. To work this increase, simply place the right-hand needle under this strand from the back and then knit it. When two stitches are to be increased along a sleeve "seam", knit one or two stitches between the increases to space them out and give the best appearance.

Decreasing. The simplest decrease is to knit two stitches together, called k2tog. This method makes the decrease slant to the right. Another decrease method is to slip one stitch without knitting it, knit the next stitch, and then pass the slip stitch over the knit stitch, called sl 1, k1, psso. This method makes the decrease slant to the left. These two decreases are essentially mirror images of each other and are generally used in tandem, one to make the shape the right side and the other to shape the left side of the garment.

Binding off. To bind off all stitches, for instance at the top of a sleeve, do as follows: Knit two stitches and then pass the first stitch (the one on the right side) over the second. Knit a third stitch and then pass the second stitch (the one on the right side) over it. Knit a fourth stitch and then pass the third (the one to the right side) over it. Continue in this way until only one stitch remains on the needle. Break the yarn and pull the tail through this last stitch.

Knitting through the back loop. Each stitch you knit is actually a piece of yarn looped over a needle. By making a knit stitch, you pull the yarn through the loop on the needle, going into the loop from left to right. If you go into the loop from right to left, you knit through the back loop, making a twisted stitch.

Purling through the back loop. With the yarn in front of the right needle, go behind the loop on the left needle and into it from left to right and pick up the strand from the front.

Purling through the back loop: Insert the right needle into the stitch from behind, then follow the arrow with the needle point.

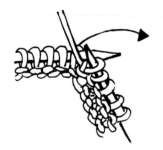

Slip the stitch off the left needle.

Weaving in loose ends. You can weave in the loose ends with a tapestry needle after you have finished knitting, or you can weave in the ends as you knit. If you choose the latter method and knit continental style (called "picking"), keep the working yarn to the right on your left index finger, and the

tail end to the left (closer to your knuckle). Knit by going alternately over and under the short end. Repeat this five or six times to fasten the tail. Before you cut off the end, pull that row of knitting sideways a little to adjust the tension.

If you knit the English way (called "throwing"), flip the tail ends alternately over and under the yarn. Then finish off in the manner described above.

Use these techniques to avoid long loops on the back when working a two-color design that has more than seven consecutive stitches in the same color.

Grafting/Kitchener stitch. Grafting is a way to join the shoulders of a garment without binding off the stitches first. It gives

Kitchener stitch: Sew through one stitch from one needle and then one stitch from the other needle as shown.

a more elastic join than traditional seaming. Leave the stitches to be joined on two needles held parallel to each other. Using an appropriate color of yarn threaded on a tapestry needle, sew through one stitch from one needle and then one stitch from the other needle, mimicking the path taken by the yarn in a knit row. The result should look like a knitted row, as shown in the drawing.

Another way to join the shoulders is to knit them together from the purl side. To do so, place the needles holding the stitches parallel to each other and then use a third knitting needle to knit two stitches togeth-

er—one stitch from each needle. When you have all the stitches on one needle, bind them off as described in "Binding off", above.

Charted Patterns. On the pattern charts, the main color is usually shown as an open square, the contrast color as a dark circle or other symbol. In reading the pattern directions, you will find the word "repeat". One repeat is the smallest unit in a design. Usually, the same unit is repeated several times—back and forth or up and down—to form a design. Sometimes the repeats do not come out even with the number of stitches you have. If this happens on the body, you should terminate the design at the side "seams" and knit one or more stitches—called marking stitches—using the darkest color in the design. On the sleeves, knit one or more marking stitches under the sleeve (as a "seam"). Place the sleeve increases on each side of the "seam" stitches.

To get a nice, even look, make sure you are consistent in the way you pick up the different colors, i.e., always pick up the pattern color from *under* the background color. If you are doing a design where you knit the same number of stitches in each of two colors, such as vertical stripes, consistency is even more important.

Duplicate stitching. Duplicate stitching is recommended for designs that require more than two colors in a row or that require single stitches of one color separated by many stitches of another color. The duplicate stitch is an embroidery technique that is worked after the piece has been knit. This stitch looks like a knitted stitch, forming Vs stacked inside one another when worked in vertical columns. To make this stitch, thread a tapestry needle with yarn. Bring the needle from the back of the knitted fabric to the knit side at the point—the base of the V—of a stitch, behind the stitch in the next row up, and then back to the purl side at the point where you started. Repeat as necessary from right to left or bottom to top.

Duplicate stitching offers many decorative possibilities that regular two-color knitting does not. You can, for example, work a design based on a cross-stitch pattern. Large areas worked in duplicate stitch look best if a slightly thinner yarn is used.

Buttonholes. Buttonholes can be made in different ways. The most common method is to bind off a certain number of stitches in one row and then cast on the same number of stitches in the next. Alternatively, you can slip the buttonhole stitches onto a piece of scrap yarn, and when you finish knitting, pull out the scrap piece and use a tapestry needle to run yarn through the live buttonhole stitches a couple times. To finish off, sew buttonhole stitches all the way around the buttonhole.

Neck openings. Many patterns require that stitches be bound off for the front and back neck openings before the garment reaches full length. You can do this two ways:

1. After you have bound off the front neck stitches, maintain the design while working back and forth until it's time to bind off for the back neck. From this point, you must finish the right and the left sides separately, working each piece back and forth.

2. To knit in the round all the way to the shoulders, make steeks on the rounds following the bind-off rounds. To work a steek, bind off for the front neck as described in the instructions, and on the next round, cast on 3 new stitches over the bound-off stitches.

Continue to work in the round, purling these new stitches every round with both strands of yarn used in each round (main color plus contrast color). Work in the round until it's time to bind off for the back neck opening, and then repeat the process.

After finishing the body of the garment, machine stitch lines of stitches on each side of the center purl stitch, and then cut the garment open between the machine stitches. Finally, pick up the appropriate number of stitches around the neck opening and work the ribbing or facing according to pattern instructions. Use this technique whenever an opening is required in the garment (center front, armhole, neck), but you prefer to knit in the round.

Facings and hems. Facings are needed to cover the cut edges when steeks are used at the top of the sleeves and around the neck. Start the sleeve facing by purling one round to mark the beginning of the facing and to provide a guide for placing the sleeve seam. To purl a complete round, simply turn the work inside out and knit the round instead. Then turn the work right side out again and finish working the specified number of rounds for the facing.

When knitting a facing for a square neck, you must increase one stitch at each corner every round to make the facing lay flat when you turn it to the inside. If you make facings for a square corner, like the lower front corner of a cardigan, you must decrease rather than increase to obtain the right shape.

Many of our designs call for a hem instead of ribbing to finish off the body or sleeves. Work a hem as the facing described above.

Finishing. In most patterns, the body and the sleeves are knitted separately in the round and then the sleeves are sewn to the body as part of the finishing. To assemble a garment, mark the sides of the body and measure the width of the sleeve. Measure this distance down from the shoulder edges to mark the position of the sleeve opening. Use thread that contrasts with the sweater to baste a guide line along the sleeve opening. Machine stitch along a single column of stitches down to the marker, across one stitch (and your basting), and then up on the other side to the shoulder. Machine stitch another line, close to the first one, to ensure that the piece won't ravel. For the machine stitches, use a three-stitch zigzag if your machine can do so. If not, use short stitches. Prevent the knitted fabric from stretching while machine stitching. For a cardigan, machine stitch twice on each side of the center front. Then cut the fabric open between the stitching and graft or knit the shoulders together as described on page 10.

After the sleeve openings have been cut, hold the sleeves next to the body, right sides together, and hand-stitch the sleeves in place using yarn. Stitch just inside the bind-off round, or into the purl round if a facing was made. On the body, stitch just inside the machine stitching. If a facing was made, fold it over the cut edge and slip stitch it to the body. Sew other facings or hems to the purl side. Work the neck according to the pattern. Weave all loose ends to the back of the fabric, and steam lightly under a damp cloth.

Through the years, many books have been written about knitting techniques. It is an extensive subject—there are many ways to cast on, bind off, increase, and decrease. We've covered only the techniques you'll need to knit the patterns in this book.

—If I wear my tights, can I wear my shorts?
—Can I wear my sandals if I put Daddy's boots over them?

When signs of spring have barely appeared,
the little girls feel a tingling in their bodies and dream of summer.
Our cool climate restricts small girls who want to wear sneakers and
knee-highs in March. But a floral wool sweater provides a happy
compromise. The designs and colors are as lush and delightful
as the summer itself. But knit with wool, the garments are both
warm and sensible. Equipped with these refreshing garments,
the summer may take as long as it wants to arrive,
or maybe not at all.

MODEL 1

Yellow Pullover with Pants and Hat

Sizes: 1 (2) 3 years

Finished Measurements:

Chest: 23$\frac{1}{2}$" (24$\frac{1}{2}$") 25$\frac{1}{4}$"

Length, pullover: 13" (14$\frac{1}{2}$") 15"

Waist, pants: 19$\frac{1}{2}$" (21") 21$\frac{1}{2}$"

Head circumference: 17" (18") 19$\frac{1}{4}$"

Yarn: Rauma Finullgarn

Yellow-gold #450; 150 (150) 150g

Light Rose #465; 100 (100) 100g

Dark Green #494; 50 (50) 50g

Purple #4088; 50 (50) 50g

Light Green #455; 50 (50) 50g

Dark Rose #456—*Pullover:* 50 (50) 50g; *Pants:* 150 (200) 250g.

Gauge: 27 sts and 32 rnds over pattern = 4 × 4 inches. Make a swatch to assure proper gauge.

Needle suggestion: Circular and double-point knitting needles size 2 and 3 (2.5mm and 3mm), or size to obtain gauge.

Body: Using smaller circular needle and Dark Rose, cast on 164 (168) 176 sts. Join, being careful not to twist sts. Knit 7 rnds for the facing, purl 1 rnd, then knit 3 rnds. Change to larger needle and work Border 1 according to the chart. The rnd starts at the left side: Mark 1 st on each side of the body (marking sts). Work the marking sts as

follows: 2 rnds Dark Rose, 14 rnds Light Green, and 2 rnds Dark Rose. Work Border 2 according to the chart, working the marking sts in Yellow on every rnd. Work Border 3 according to the chart, working the marking sts in the color of your choice—they will be cut open later for the sleeve openings. Shape front neck by binding off 31 (33) 35 sts at center front according to the chart. On the next rnd, cast on 2 sts over bound-off sts. Purl the 2 new sts using both colors. Continue Border 3 until full length for your size, finishing with 1 Purple rnd. Bind off remaining sts or put them on holders.

Sleeves: Make 2. Using smaller double-point needles and Dark Rose, cast on 50 (50) 52 sts. Join, being careful not to twist sts. Knit 7 rnds for facing, then purl 1 rnd, and knit 5 rnds. Change to larger needles. Make the first st on the rnd the marking st, and work it in Yellow every rnd, working incs at underarm on each side of this st. Work Border 2 according to the chart. After 5 (4) 4 rnds of Border 2, start underarm incs as follows: Size 1 year: Inc 2 sts every 4th rnd 12 times, then 2 sts after the 5th rnd just once. Size 2 years: Inc 2 sts every 3rd rnd 8 times, then every 4th rnd 8 times. Size 3 years: Inc 2 sts every 3rd rnd 10 times, then every 4th rnd 8 times. Work Border 1 without increasing. The marking st is worked in the same color as worked on the body. To finish, knit 2 rnds, then purl 1 rnd. Using Purple, knit 5 rnds for facing. Bind off.

Finishing: For details on finishing, see Knitting Techniques on page 11. Machine stitch and cut for sleeve and neck openings. Sew or graft the shoulders together. Using smaller needle and Dark Rose, pick up the sts around the neck. Join, being careful not to twist sts. Knit 3 rnds, decreasing 1 st at each

corner of the neck band each rnd. Purl 1 rnd. Knit 5 rnds for facing, increasing 1 st at each corner each rnd. Bind off. Sew in sleeves. Weave all loose ends into the back of the fabric and slip stitch the facings to the wrong side. Steam lightly.

Pants: Start at the lower edge of one leg. Using smaller double-point needles and Purple, cast on 56 (60) 64 sts. Join, being careful not to twist sts. Knit 7 rnds for facing, then purl 1 rnd, and knit 2 rnds. Change to larger needles and work Border 1. The first st on each rnd is the marking st, and is worked in the same colors as worked on the body. After Border 1, change to Dark Rose. On the next rnd, inc evenly spaced to 88 (96) 104 sts and work until the leg measures 11" (12$\frac{1}{2}$") 13$\frac{3}{4}$" from the purl rnd. Set aside, and knit the other leg. Put the sts from both legs, a total of 176 (192) 208 sts, on a circular needle. Mark the 2 center front and the two center back sts, and dec 1 st on each side of these center sts every other rnd 6 times—152 (168) 184 sts remain. When the pants measure 8$\frac{1}{4}$" (9$\frac{3}{8}$") 10$\frac{1}{4}$" from the crotch, work as follows: Start at center back and k30 sts. Turn, slip the first st and p60 sts. Turn, slip the first st and k55 sts. Turn, slip the first st and continue working 5 sts fewer each row until 20 sts remain at center back. Knit 1 rnd (over all the sts), decreasing evenly spaced to 144 (154) 164 sts. Change to smaller needle and work k1, p1 ribbing for 2$\frac{1}{4}$". Bind off. Fold the waist band and slip stitch to the wrong side leaving a small opening for elastic. Insert elastic, measuring 19$\frac{5}{8}$" (20$\frac{7}{8}$") 21$\frac{5}{8}$" long. Sew the leg facings to the wrong side. Steam lightly.

Hat: Check your gauge. A small difference in gauge can make a big difference in the finished size. Using smaller circular needle and Purple, cast on 116 (124) 132 sts. Join, being careful not to twist sts. Knit 7 rnds for facing, purl 1 rnd, and knit 2 rnds. Change to larger needle and work Border 1. Work 1 marking st at the beginning of the rnd in the same color as worked on the body. Change to Dark Rose and inc 4 sts evenly spaced in the first rnd. Place 8 markers on the rnd with 15 (16) 17 sts between markers. Inc 1 st after each marker every 3rd rnd 3 times. Knit 9 rnds without increasing. Now dec 1 st after each marker every other rnd until 16 sts remain. Thread remaining sts on yarn and gather. Weave all loose ends into the back of the fabric. Make a Purple pom-pom and sew to the top of the hat. Sew the facing to the wrong side.

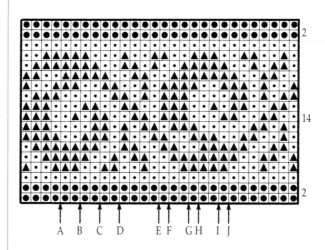

Border 1
The letters indicate where to start.

A: Pants 1 year
B: Pants 2 years, hat 1 year
C: Pants 3 years
D: Hat 2 years
E: Hat 3 years
F: Sleeve 1 year
G: Body 1 year
H: Body 2 years, sleeve 2 years
I: Body 3 years
J: Sleeve 3 years

MODEL 1

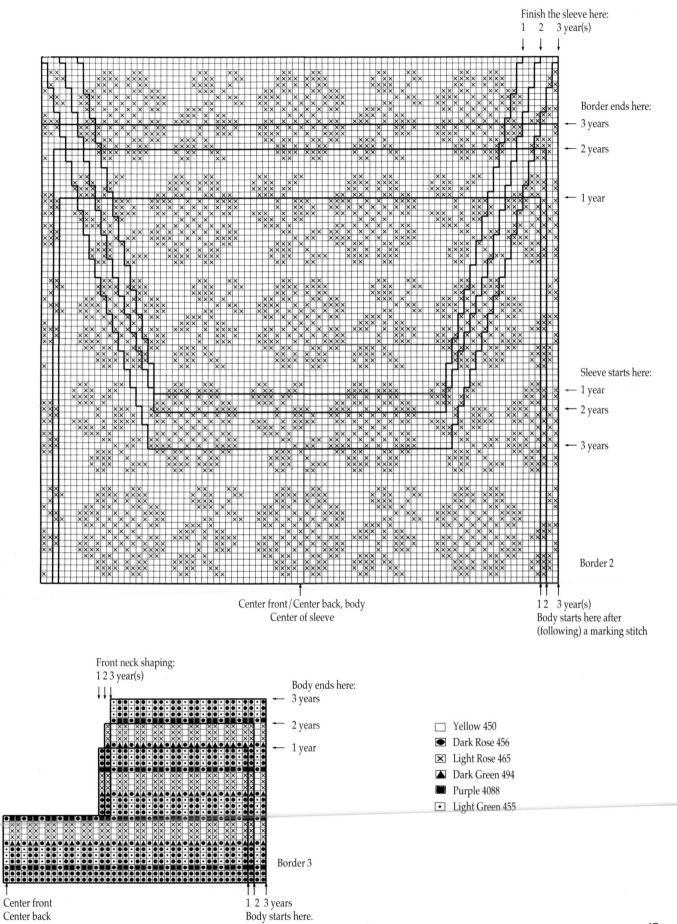

Finish the sleeve here:
1 2 3 year(s)

Border ends here:
← 3 years
← 2 years
← 1 year

Sleeve starts here:
← 1 year
← 2 years
← 3 years

Border 2

Center front / Center back, body
Center of sleeve

1 2 3 year(s)
Body starts here after
(following) a marking stitch

Front neck shaping:
1 2 3 year(s)

Body ends here:
← 3 years
← 2 years
← 1 year

☐ Yellow 450
◉ Dark Rose 456
☒ Light Rose 465
▲ Dark Green 494
■ Purple 4088
⊡ Light Green 455

Border 3

Center front
Center back

1 2 3 years
Body starts here.

MODEL 2

Tulip

Sizes: 2 (4) 6 years

Finished Measurements:

Chest: 26¾" (30⅝") 33"

Length, dress: 18½" (21¼") 23¼"

Length, tights 21¼" (24⅜") 27½"

Head circumference 20⅜" for all sizes

Yarn: Rauma Finullgarn

Dress:

Orange #469; 150 (200) 250g

Dark Rose #4886; 50 (50) 50g

Light Rose #4686; 50 (100) 100g

Medium Green #430; 50 (50) 50g

Light Green #493; 100 (100) 100g

Yellow #450; 50 (50) 50g

Tights:

Orange #469; 50 (50) 100g

Dark Rose #4886; 50 (50) 100g

Light Rose #4686; 50 (50) 100g

Medium Green #430; 50 (50) 100g

Light Green #493; 50 (50) 100g

Yellow #450; 50 (50) 50g

Black #436; 50 (50) 50g

Gauge: 27 sts and 32 rows over pattern = 4 × 4 inches. Make a swatch to assure proper gauge.

Needle suggestion: Double-point and circular needles size 2 and 3 (2.5mm and 3mm), or size to obtain gauge.

Dress: Using larger needle and Orange, cast on 182 (210) 224 sts. Join, being careful not to twist sts. Work Border 1 according to the chart until the dress measures 13¾" (16½") 18½". Bind off center front 21 (25) 27 sts for neck opening. Work back and forth in stockinette stitch. Dec 1 st on the neck side every other row for 2". Then bind off center back 37 (41) 43 sts for back neck opening. Finish each side separately, working each for 3/4". Bind off remaining sts or put them on a holder.

Sleeves: Make 2. Using larger needle and Orange, cast on 35 (39) 41 sts. Join, being careful not to twist sts. Work Border 1, and *at the same time* inc 2 sts at underarm every other rnd until there are 89 (109) 113 sts. Work until the sleeve measures 9¾" (11⅜") 13¾". Purl 6 rnds for the facing, increasing 2 sts at underarm every rnd. Bind off.

Finishing: For details on finishing, see Knitting Techniques on page 11. Machine stitch and cut open for sleeves. Sew or graft the shoulders together. Using Yellow, pick up sts around the neck and work lace border in the rnd: Knit 2 rnds, then "picot edge" as follows: *yarn over, k2tog, k3; rep from * around. Knit 1 rnd working 6 sts (alternate k1, p1) into each yarn over of the previous rnd. Purl 1 rnd, bind off. Work the same lace border on each cuff. Using Light Rose, pick up sts around the lower edge of the dress, and work lace border: Knit 1 rnd, then "picot edge" as follows: *K2tog, k4, yarn over; rep from * around. Knit 1 rnd working 2 sts (k1, p1) into each yarn over from the previous rnd. Work another "picot rnd": *K2tog, k3, yarn over, k2tog, yarn over; rep from * around. Knit 1 rnd working 2 sts; k1, p1, into each yarn over of the previous rnd. *K2tog, k2, yarn over, k2tog, k3, yarn over; rep from * around. Knit 1 rnd working 2 sts (k1, p1) into each yarn over of the previous rnd. *K2tog, k1, yarn over, k6, yarn over; rep from * around. Knit 1 rnd working 2 sts (k1, p1) into each yarn over of the previous rnd. *K2tog, yarn over, k2tog, k9, yarn over; rep from * around. Knit 1 rnd working 2 sts (k1, p1) into each yarn over of the previous rnd. *K2tog, k13, yarn over; rep from * around. Change to Yellow. Purl 1 rnd and bind off. Sew in the sleeves. Weave all loose ends into the back of the fabric and sew the facings to the wrong side. Steam lightly. Option: Sew Pink beads on the flowers.

Tights: Using smaller needle and Orange, cast on 144 (152) 164 sts. Join, being careful not to twist sts. Work for 1⅛" (casing for elastic), purl 1 rnd, knit for 1⅛". Change to larger needle and work k2, p2 ribbing in a stripe design: *Orange 8 rnds, Medium Green 2 rnds, Light Green 4 rnds, Yellow 2 rnds, Dark Rose 4 rnds, Black 2 rnds, Light Rose 4 rnds, Yellow 2 rnds; repeat from *. When the tights measures 7⅞" (8⅝") 9⅜" from the purl rnd, inc 2 sts at center front and center back every other rnd until there are 160 (168) 176 sts. Put 80 (84) 88 sts—from center front to center back—on a holder.

Work in the rnd over remaining sts (one leg). At the inseam, dec 2 sts every 4th rnd 12 (14) 14 times. Then dec 2 sts every 6th (9th) 12th rnd 7 (6) 6 times. Work until the leg measures 11³⁄₈" (13³⁄₄") 16¹⁄₈", or desired length. Using Orange, knit for 1¹⁄₈" and bind off. Work the other leg the same. Sew the facings to the wrong side, and put in elastic at the waistband.

Hat: Check your gauge. A small difference in gauge can make a big difference in the finished size. Using smaller needle and Yellow, cast on 140 sts. Join, being careful not to twist sts. Knit for 1¹⁄₈" for facing, then make a "picot edge": *Yarn over, k2tog; repeat from * around. Knit 2 rnds. Change to Orange. Work one leaf and flower repeat. Continue using Orange only, increasing as follows: *K4, inc 1; rep from * around. Knit 6 rnds. *K5, inc 1; rep from * around. Knit 6 rnds. *K6, inc 1; rep from * around. Knit 6 rnds. Purl 1 rnd, purling 50 of the sts onto scrap yarn. This yarn will later on be removed to get sts for the long tip of the hat. Continue knitting in stockinette stitch, following the same stripe design as on the tights. Knit 6 rnds, then start decreasing:

*K6, dec 1; rep from * around. Knit 6 rnds. *K5, dec 1; rep from * around. Knit 6 rnds. *K4, dec 1; rep from * around. Knit 6 rnds. *K3, dec 1; rep from * around. Knit 6 rnds. *K3, dec 1; rep from * around. Knit 6 rnds. *K2, dec 1; rep from * around. Knit 6 rnds. *K2, dec 1; rep from * around. Knit 6 rnds. *K1, dec 1; rep from * around. Knit 6 sts. K2tog around. Put remaining sts on yarn,

gather, and fasten off. Pick out the scrap yarn, and work the stripe design in the rnd, decreasing 2 sts on each side every 4th rnd until 10 sts remain. Put remaining sts on yarn, gather, and fasten off. Make a Yellow pompom and sew to the top of the hat. Steam lightly. Option: Sew beads on the flowers.

↑ Border 1
Start here on the side for all sizes.

☐ Orange 469
▲ Light Green 493
▼ Medium Green 430
◉ Light Rose 4686
● Dark Rose 4886

MODEL 3

Floral Pullover

Sizes: 10 (12) 14 years

Finished Measurements:

Chest: 39³⁄₈" (39³⁄₈") 39³⁄₈"

Length: 16⁷⁄₈" (17¹⁄₄") 17³⁄₄"

Length from cuff to cuff: 58¹⁄₄" (59⁷⁄₈") 62¹⁄₄"

Head circumference: 20³⁄₈" for all sizes

Yarn: Rauma Finullgarn

Charcoal #4387; 300 (350) 400)g

Light Green #493; 100 (100) 150g

Medium Green #430; 100 (100) 150g

Dark Rose #4886; 50 (50) 50g

Red #439; 50 (50) 50g

Light Rose #4686; 50 (50) 50g

Yellow #431; 50 (50) 50)g

Gauge: 27 sts and 32 rows over pattern = 4 × 4 inches. Make a swatch to assure proper gauge.

Needle suggestion: Double-point and circular needles size 3 (3mm), or size to obtain gauge.

Note: This pullover is knit from cuff to cuff. Neck and bottom openings are cut open when finishing.

Pullover: Using Yellow, cast on 43 (45) 49 sts. Join, being careful not to twist sts. Work for 1¹⁄₈", then make a "picot edge": *Yarn over, k2tog; rep from * around. Knit 2 rnds. Start Border 1. Make the first st on the rnd the marking st, working it in Charcoal every rnd. After 1¹⁄₈", inc 1 st on each side of the marking st every other rnd until there are 77 (79) 81 sts. Then inc 1 st on each side of the marking st every rnd until there are 231 (235) 237 sts. Work until the sleeve measures 19¹⁄₄" (20") 21¹⁄₄". At an appropriate place in the repeat, start working the design for the body, starting with Border 2. *At the same time,* cast on 3 sts over the marking st. Purl these 3 sts every rnd using both strands. They are for machine stitching and cutting later on. Work Border 2, 4 floral repeats, 1 center repeat, and 4 floral repeats mirror imaged, which finishes the body. To start the other sleeve, bind off the 3 purl sts and then work the marking st in Charcoal. Work down the sleeve, decreasing on each side of the marking st, where you increased for the first sleeve. When a total of 43 (45) 49 sts remain, knit 1¹⁄₈" without decreasing, then work the "picot edge" and the facing as before. Bind off.

Finishing: Machine stitch and cut open for the bottom opening in the double-strand purl sts. If you find it difficult to sew through the cuff opening, cut a small hole at the bottom, near the marking st first, big enough to fit the sewing machine foot into, to make it easier to do the machine stitching. For the boat neck opening, baste along the top row. The neck opening is positioned over the center repeat and 1 floral repeat to each side of the center. Fasten off the basting thread on each side so the knitting does not stretch when machine stitching. Machine stitch and cut. Using Yellow, pick up sts around the neck opening. Knit 2 rnds, make a "picot edge", and knit 1¹⁄₈" for facing. Bind off. Using Yellow, pick up sts around the lower edge and finish off as around the neck. Weave all loose ends into the back of the fabric, sew the facings to the wrong side, and steam lightly.

Hat: Check your gauge. A small difference in gauge can make a big difference in the finished size. Using Yellow, cast on 140 sts. Join, being careful not to twist sts. Knit 4" for facing. Make a "picot edge": *Yarn over, k2tog; rep from * around. Knit 2 rnds. Work the center repeat from the pullover. Using Charcoal, knit 1 rnd, using Green #493, purl 2 rnds, then continue using Charcoal, decreasing as follows: *Dec 1, k6; rep from * around. Knit 5 rnds. *Dec 1, k5; rep from * around. Knit 5 rnds. *Dec 1, k4; rep from * around. Knit 5 rnds. *Dec 1, k3; repeat from * around. Knit 5 rnds. *Dec 1, k2; rep from * around. Knit 5 rnds. *Dec 1, k1; rep from * around. K2tog around. Put remaining sts on yarn, gather, and fasten off. Weave all loose ends into the back of the fabric, sew the facings to the wrong side, and steam lightly.

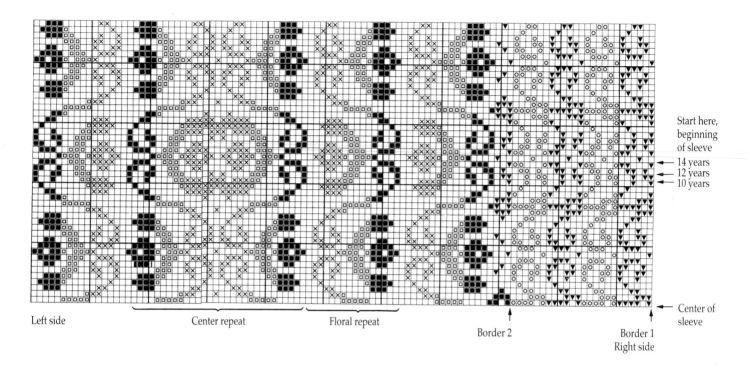

Start here,
beginning
of sleeve

← 14 years
← 12 years
← 10 years

← Center of
sleeve

Left side

Center repeat

Floral repeat

Border 2

Border 1
Right side

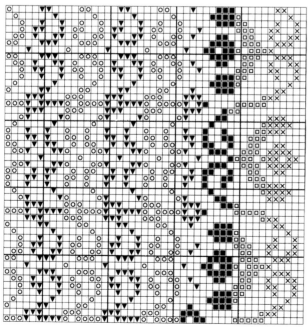

☐ Charcoal 4387

☒ Light Rose 4686

◉ Light Green 493

▼ Medium Green 430

■ Dark Rose 4886

⊡ Red 439

Left side continues

Floral Cardigan

Sizes: 10 (12) 14 years

Finished Measurements:

Chest: 37¾" (42½") 42½"

Length: 17¾" (19⅝") 21⅝"

Head circumference: (20⅜") 22"

Yarn: Rauma Finullgarn

Black #436; 250 (300) 300g

Orange #469; 50 (100) 100g

Rose #4886; 50 (100) 100g

Dark Rust #419; 50 (100) 100g

Light Rust #434; 50 (100) 100g

Olive #489; 50 (50) 50g

Gauge: 27 sts and 32 rows over pattern = 4 × 4 inches. Make a swatch to assure proper gauge.

Needle suggestion: Double-point and circular needles size 2 and 3 (2.5mm and 3mm) or size to obtain gauge.

Body: Using smaller needle and Black, cast on 200 (220) 240 sts. Join, being careful not to twist sts. Knit for 3/4". Change to larger needle and inc evenly spaced to 258 (290) 290 sts. Purl the 2 center front sts using both strands on all rnds. They are for machine stitching and cutting later on. Work Border 1 according to the chart. The main color changes every rnd between Rust #434, Orange, Rust #419, and Rose. Work until the body measures full length, and bind off.

Sleeves: Make 2. Using smaller needles and Black, cast on 40 (42) 44 sts. Join, being

25

careful not to twist sts. Knit for 3/4". Change to larger needles and inc evenly spaced to 51 (57) 63 sts. Make the first st on the rnd the marking st, and work it in Black every rnd. Work Border 1 increasing 1 st on each side of the marking st every other rnd until there are 125 (135) 145 sts. Work until the sleeve measures 16⅞" (18½") 19⅝". Purl 6 rnds for facing, increasing 2 sts at underarm every rnd. Bind off.

Finishing: For details on finishing, see Knitting Techniques on page 11. Machine stitch and cut for sleeve openings. The neck opening measures 40 sts wide, 2" deep at center front, and 3/4" deep at center back. Shape the neckline by basting, machine stitching, and cutting. Sew the shoulders. Using circular needle and Black, pick up sts around the lower edge, along both front edges, and around the neck in one piece. Using Olive, work a lace border: Knit 2 rnds. *Yarn over, k2tog, k3; rep from * around. Knit 1 rnd, working 6 sts, alternately k1, p1, into each yarn over from the previous rnd. Purl 1 rnd. Bind off. Work the same lace border around each cuff. Sew in the sleeves. Weave all loose ends into the back of the fabric, and steam lightly. If you prefer closures for the cardigan, we suggest using eyes and hooks sewn to the inside.

Border 1
Center front.
Start all
sizes here

Hat: 10/12 (14) years. Check your gauge. A small difference in the gauge can make a big difference in the finished size. Using smaller needle and Olive, cast on 140 (150) sts. Join, being careful not to twist sts. Knit 1⅛" in the rnd for facing. Next rnd: *yarn over, k2tog; rep from * around. Knit 2 rnds. Change to Black and knit 3/4". Change to larger needle, increasing to 160 (192) sts. Work until the hat measures 7⅞" from the yarn over rnd. Put remaining sts on yarn, gather, and fasten off. Weave all loose ends into the back of the fabric, sew the facing to the wrong side, and steam lightly. Make a Black pompom and sew to the top of the hat.

☐ Alternate 1 rnd
  each color:
  Light Rust 434
  Orange 469
  Dark Rust 419
  Rose 4886

■ Black

Some golden moments with children keep their luster for years to come. Usually it is not visits to amusement parks or the excitement over expensive Christmas gifts that we remember best, but the small, everyday experiences:

—a bouquet of yellow flowers delivered with love and triumph

—a thoughtful chat on the porch swing one spring evening

—a joint effort baking bread without fuss about flour on the floor and dough on the clothes

—a swim in water that's just a little too cool one spring afternoon

—riotous play among the fall leaves in the park in October

—biking to the store with a six-year-old who has just learned to ride.

We can get many such memories by taking time for hikes in the woods, baking days, and trips to the shore. Wool outfits and thin windbreakers are just as practical as thick snow suits when hiking. Many thin, but warm layers make it easier to adjust the body temperature as needed. A thick snow suit and just one layer of thin clothing underneath give only two options—warm or cold. Hardly anything can feel more hopeless for a little one than to stand—all sweaty —at the bottom of a hill. In that case, Mom and Dad have to wait a long time for those golden moments, especially if they are at the top of the hill themselves and start walking as soon as the little one catches up with them, warm as toast and out of breath . . .

MODEL 5

A Cardigan for the Smallest Ones

Sizes: Newborn (3 months) 6 months

Finished Measurements:

Chest: 19⁵/₈" (20³/₈") 21¹/₄"

Length: 9¹/₂" (10¹/₄") 10³/₄"

Yarn: Røros Lamullgarn

Wine #48

Cardigan, hat and socks: 150 (150) 150g

Cardigan only: 100 (100) 150g

Gauge: 28 sts and 56 rows garter st (56 rows = 28 "ridges") = 4 × 4 inches; 36 sts and 48 rows over ribbing = 4 × 4 inches. Make a swatch to assure proper fit.

Needle suggestion: Short circular needles size 0 and 2 (2mm and 2.5mm), or size to obtain gauge.

Body: The cardigan is worked back and forth in one piece. Using smaller needle, cast on 136 (144) 148 sts. Work k1, p1 ribbing for 12 (13) 14 rows. Change to larger needle and work garter st until the body measures 4³/₄" (5¹/₈") 5¹/₂". Place one marker after 33 (35) 36 sts, and another marker before the last 33 (35) 36 sts. Bind off 6 (8) 8 sts for sleeve openings between the fronts and the back (where the markers are). Put work aside and knit the sleeves.

Sleeves: Make 2. Using smaller needle, cast on 44 (48) 50 sts and work k1, p1 ribbing back and forth for 12 (13) 14 rows. Change to larger needle and work garter st. Beginning on the 5th (6th) 6th row, inc 1 st after the first and before the last st every 4th (5th) 5th row 5 (13) 6 times, then every 5th (0) 6th row 8 (0) 7 times. Work until the sleeve measures 5³/₄" (6¹/₄") 6³/₄". Bind off 3 (4) 4 sts on each side.

Joining the body and the sleeves: Put the sleeves on the same needle as the body (front, sleeve, back, sleeve, front). Make sure the bound-off sts on the body and on the sleeves coincide. Place markers for raglan dec where the fronts and the sleeves meet, and where the back and the sleeves meet. Dec 1 st on each side of these markers every other row 20 (20) 21 times—92 (96) 100 sts remain. Change to smaller needle and work k1, p1 ribbing for 10 rows. Bind off. Using smaller needle, pick up sts along the front edges for front bands. Work k1, p1 ribbing for 10 rows. On the button band, make 5 buttonholes evenly spaced on the 5th row. Make each buttonhole over 1 st: yarn over, k2tog. Work k1, p1 ribbing across the 6th row, treating the yarn over from the previous row as 1 st.

Finishing: For details on finishing, see Knitting Techniques on page 11. Sew the sleeves together from the wrong side and sew the bound-off sts at underarms together. Weave all loose ends into the back of the fabric, and sew 5 buttons to the button band.

Hat: Check your gauge. A small difference in the gauge can make a big difference in the finished size. Using larger needle (or smaller needle, depending on your gauge), cast on 36 sts. Work back and forth in garter st. Knit 1 row. Dec 1 st after the 2 first sts, and inc 1 st before the 2 last sts every other row 19 times. On the next 38 rows (19 "ridges"), inc 1 st after the 2 first sts, and dec 1 st before the last 2 sts every other row. This makes one ear flap. Dec 1 st after the 2 first sts, and inc 1 st before the 2 last sts every other row 9 times. Then inc 1 st after the 2 first sts, and dec 1 st before the 2 last sts every other row 9 times. This makes the point at the forehead. Now make the other ear flap as the first one. Bind off. Sew the cast-on and the bound-off edges and the points together on the wrong side. Twist cords and sew to each ear flap. Option: Crochet 1 row single crochet around the hat using a fine crochet hook. At each ear flap, crochet chain sts for 8", turn, and work single crochet back towards the ear flap. Continue crocheting around, crocheting another band at the other ear flap.

Socks: Work the sole first, then the toe, and then the ankle.

Work back and forth and sew together when finishing. The sock is worked in garter stitch with a short ribbing at the top for elasticity.

Using larger needle, cast on 31 sts.

Row 1: Knit.

Row 2: Sl 1, k1, inc 1, k13, inc 1, k1, inc 1, k13, inc 1, k2.

Rows 3, 5, 7, and 9: Knit.

Row 4: Sl 1, k2, inc 1, k13, inc 1, k3, inc 1, k13, inc 1, k3.

Row 6: Sl 1, k3, inc 1, k13, inc 1, k5, inc 1, k13, inc 1, k4.

Row 8: Sl 1, k4, inc 1, k13, inc 1, k7, inc 1, k13, inc 1, k5.

Knit 4 "ridges", counted on the right side. K28 sts, *turn, sl the first st, k7, k2tog; repeat from * until 10 sts remain on each side. Knit 3 rows. Make holes for cord: *k1, yarn over, k2tog; repeat from * across. Knit 18 "ridges". Finish by working k1, p1 ribbing for 7 rows. Bind off loosely. Make the other sock the same.

Finishing: Sew the sock together from the wrong side. Thread a twisted cord, a silk ribbon, or elastic through the holes. Fold the top edge over to make it double.

MODEL 6

Reindeer Pullover for the Hunting Season

Sizes: 1 (2) 3 years

Finished Measurements:

Chest: 29$\frac{1}{8}$" (30$\frac{1}{4}$") 31$\frac{1}{8}$"

Length, pullover: 12$\frac{1}{2}$" (14") 15"

Waist, pants: 19$\frac{5}{8}$" (20$\frac{7}{8}$") 21$\frac{5}{8}$"

Head circumference: 16$\frac{7}{8}$" (18$\frac{1}{8}$") 19$\frac{1}{4}$"

Yarn: Rauma Finullgarn

Pullover:

Dark Blue #447; 150 (150) 200g

Light Rose #4087; 50 (50) 50g

Light Purple #473; 50 (50) 50g

Old Rose #490; 50 (50) 50g

Dark Rose #466; 50 (50) 50g

Jade #4887; 50 (50) 50g

Light Green #493; 50 (50) 50g

Steel Blue #451; 50 (50) 50g

Pants:

Dark Blue #447; 150 (200) 250g

Leftover yarn from the pullover for embroidery.

Gauge: 27 sts and 32 rows over pattern = 4 × 4 inches; 34 sts and 38 rows over ribbing = 4 × 4 inches. Make a swatch to assure proper gauge.

Needle suggestion: Double-point and circular needles size 2 and 3 (2.5mm and 3mm), or size to obtain gauge.

Body: Using smaller needle and Dark Blue, cast on 200 (208) 216 sts. Join, being careful not to twist sts. Work k1, p1 ribbing for 8 (8) 9 rnds. Change to larger needle. Knit 1 rnd. Change to Dark Rose and knit 2 rnds. Make 1 st on each side the marking sts and work them in Dark Blue every rnd. Work Border 1 on the front and on the back. Color changes and dec are marked on the chart. Work until A for your size on the chart, and then bind off 6 (7) 8 sts on each side according to the chart. Set the body aside and start the sleeves.

Sleeves: Make 2. Using smaller needles and Dark Blue, cast on 50 (52) 54 sts. Join, being careful not to twist sts. Work 8 (8) 9 rnds of k1, p1 ribbing, then knit 1 rnd. Change to Dark Rose and knit 2 rnds. The first st on the rnd is the marking st, and is worked in Dark Blue every rnd. Work incs on each side of this st. Change to larger needles and work Border 2. Color changes and incs are marked on the chart. Work until A for your size on the chart and bind off the number of sts indicated on the chart.

Raglan shaping: Put the body and the sleeves on the same needle. Make sure the decs on the body and the sleeves coincide. Where the sts from the body and the sleeves meet, always knit 1 st from each part in Dark Blue (marking sts). All decs are done on each side of the marking sts, but, as shown on the charts, the decs for the body and the sleeves are not the same. After Border 1 on the body and Border 2 on the

sleeves, continue working the design, and dec according to the chart. Change to shorter circular needle or double-point needles when necessary. Finish with 2 rnds in Dark Rose. Change to smaller needle and Dark Blue. Work 16 (16) 18 rnds of k1, p1 ribbing. Bind off loosely or put remaining sts on a holder.

Finishing: For details on finishing, see Knitting Techniques on page 11. Sew the sts at underarms. Weave all loose ends into the back of the fabric. Fold the neckband and sew it to the wrong side.

Pants: Start at the lower edge of one leg. Using smaller needles and Dark Blue, cast on 56 (60) 64 sts. Join, being careful not to twist sts. Work k1, p1 ribbing for 1$\frac{1}{2}$" (2") 2". Change to larger needles and knit 1 rnd, increasing evenly spaced to 88 (96) 104 sts. Work until the leg measures 11" (12$\frac{1}{2}$") 13$\frac{3}{4}$". Make the other leg the same. Put the sts from both legs on one circular needle—a total of 176 (192) 208 sts. The 2 center front and 2 center back sts are marking sts. Dec 1 st on each side of the marking sts every other rnd 6 times—

152 (168) 184 sts remain. When the pants measure 8¼" (9⅜") 10¼" from the crotch, make them higher in the back: Starting at center back, k30, turn. Sl the first st, p60, turn. Sl the first st, k55, turn. Sl the first st and work 5 sts fewer every time you turn, until 20 sts remain at center back. Knit one rnd, decreasing evenly spaced to 144 (154) 164 sts. Change to smaller needle and work k1, p1 ribbing for 2¼". Bind off. Fold the waist band and sew to the wrong side leav-ing a small opening for elastic. After the elastic is in, the waist should measure 19⅝" (20⅞") 21⅝". Using duplicate st, sew 3 trees from Border 2 on an imaginary "pocket", using the colors from the pullover.

Hat: Check your gauge. A small differ-ence in gauge can make a big difference in the finished size. Using smaller needle and Dark Rose, cast on 116 (124) 132 sts. Knit 7 rnds for facing, purl 1 rnd, and knit 2 rnds. Change to larger needle and work Border 3 once. Change to Dark Blue and inc 4 sts evenly spaced on the first rnd. Place a mark-er every 15 (16) 17 sts—8 sections—and inc 1 st at the beginning of each section every 3rd rnd 3 times. Knit 6 rnds without incs, then dec 1 st at the beginning of each section every other rnd until 16 sts remain. Put remaining sts on yarn, gather, and fasten off. Sew the facing to the wrong side. Make a small pompom in Dark Rose and sew to the top of the hat.

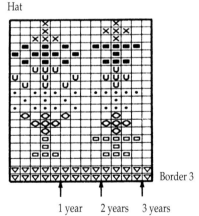

☐ Dark Blue 447
• Light Rose 4087
Ⓞ Light Purple 473
▢ Old Rose 490
▽ Dark Rose 466
Ⓤ Jade 4887
■ Light Green 493
✕ Steel Blue 451

Hat

Border 3

1 year   2 years   3 years

Body

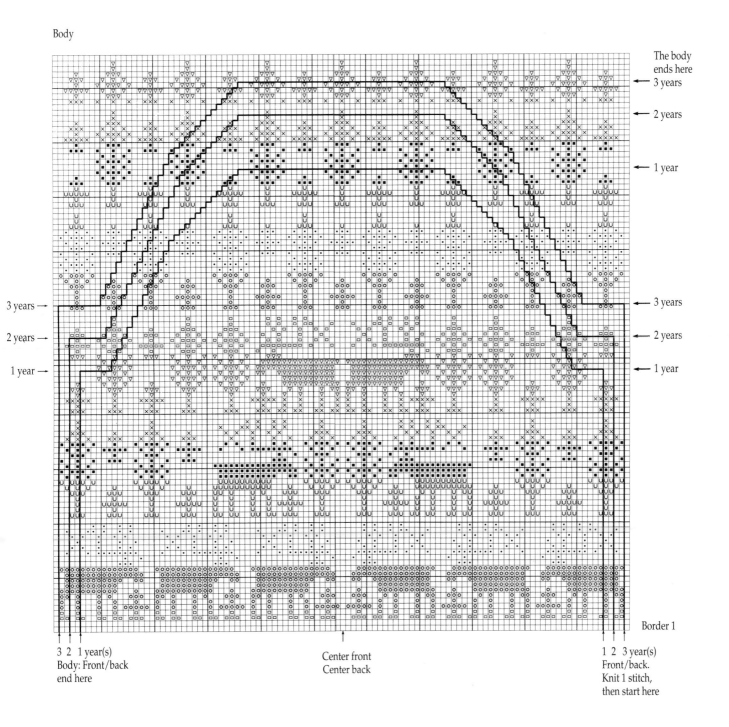

The body
ends here
← 3 years

← 2 years

← 1 year

3 years →

2 years →

1 year →

← 3 years

← 2 years

← 1 year

Border 1

3 2 1 year(s)
Body: Front/back
end here

Center front
Center back

1 2 3 year(s)
Front/back.
Knit 1 stitch,
then start here

Sleeve

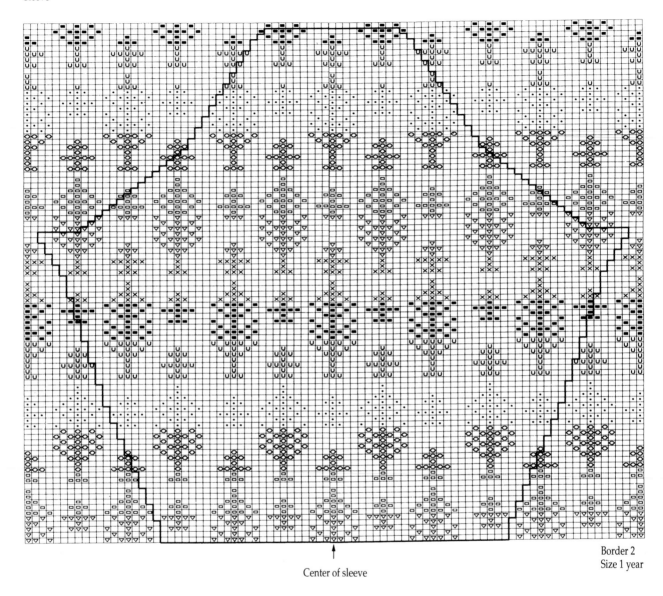

Center of sleeve

Border 2
Size 1 year

Sleeve

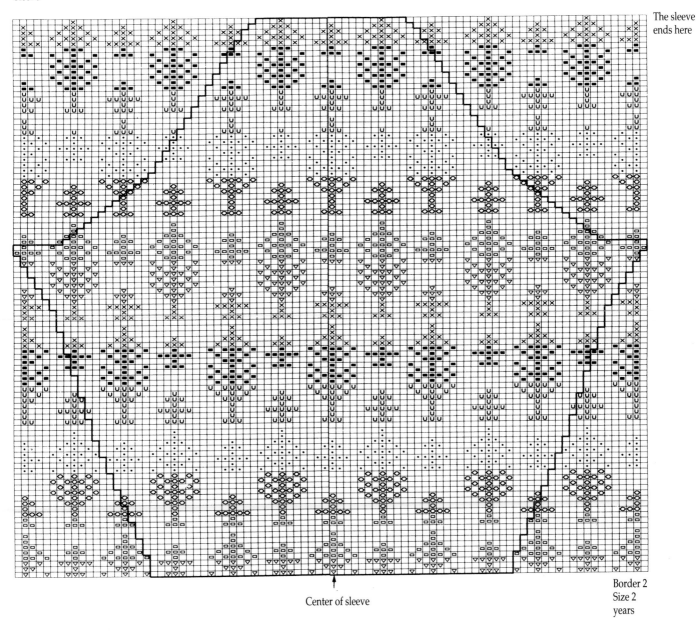

Center of sleeve

Border 2
Size 2
years

Sleeve

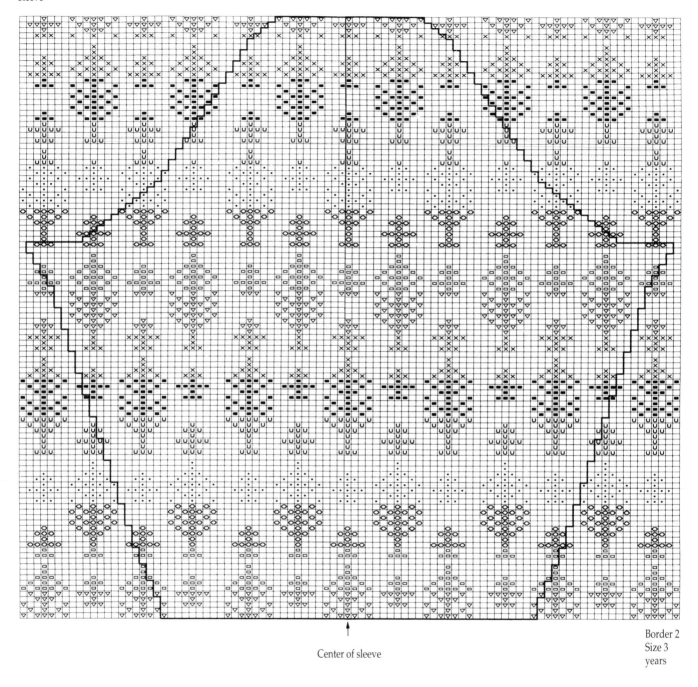

Center of sleeve

Border 2
Size 3
years

Princess Suit for Small Girls

Sizes: 1 (2) 3 years

Finished Measurements:

Chest: 23⅝" (26¾") 28¼"

Length, pullover: 12½" (13¾") 14½"

Waist, pants: 19⅝" (20⅞") 21⅝"

Yarn: Rauma Finullgarn

Colorway 1

Color 1: Old Rose #427

Pullover and pants: 50 (50) 50g

Color 2: Dark Rose #466

Pullover: 50 (100) 150g

Pants: 100 (100) 150g

Color 3: Light Rose #4571

Pullover: 100 (150) 200g

Pants: 100 (150) 150g

Colorway 2

Color 1: Clear Blue #437

Color 2: Dark Rose #439

Color 3: Light Rose #479

Gauge: 27 sts and 32 rows over pattern = 4 × 4 inches. Make a swatch to assure proper gauge.

Needle suggestion: Double-point and circular needles size 2 and 3 (2.5mm and 3mm), or size to obtain gauge.

Body: Using smaller needle and Color 1, cast on 144 (152) 160 sts. Join, being careful not to twist sts. Knit 7 rnds for facing, purl 1 rnd, and knit 3 rnds. Change to Color 2 and knit 1 rnd. The 3 sts on each side are marking sts and are worked in Color 2 every rnd.

The incs are made on each side of these sts (see below). Change to larger needle and work Border 1 on the front and Border 2 on the back. Inc 1 st on each side of the marking sts—4 sts each rnd—as follows, counted from the purl rnd: Size 1 year: Inc 4 sts after the 9th rnd, then every 9th rnd 4 times—164 sts. Size 2 years: Inc 4 sts every 5th rnd 2 times, then every 6th rnd 6 times—184 sts. Size 3 years: Inc 4 sts after the 6th rnd, then every 5th rnd 9 times—196 sts. Work the design until the body measures 5¾" (5⅞") 5⅞" from the purl rnd. Bind off the marking sts, and on the next rnd, cast on 2 new sts over the bound-off sts. Purl the new sts every rnd using both strands. They are for machine stitching and cutting later on. When the body measures 9⅜" (11⅜") 12⅛", shape for square neck by binding off center front 23 (25) 25 sts. On the next rnd, cast on 2 new sts over bound-off sts. Purl the new sts every rnd using both strands. When the body measures 11" (13") 13¾", bind off center back 23 (25) 25 sts for back neck opening. On the next rnd, cast on 2 new sts over the bound-off sts. Purl the new sts every rnd using both strands. Put all the sts on a holder, or bind off, when the body measures full length.

Sleeves: Make 2. Using smaller needle and Color 1, cast on 44 (54) 54 sts. Join, being careful not to twist sts. Knit 7 rnds for facing, then purl 1 rnd, and knit 3 rnds. Using Color 2, knit 1 rnd. Make the 3 center underarm sts the marking sts and work them in Color 2 every rnd, working the incs on each side of these sts. Change to larger needle and work Border 2. After the 3rd rnd, inc 2 sts every other rnd 10 (13) 15 times, then every 3rd rnd 16 (14) 18 times. When the sleeve measures 8¼" (9⅜") 10¼", change to Color 1.

Knit 3 rnds, purl 1 rnd, and knit 7 rnds for facing. Bind off.

Finishing: For details on finishing, see Knitting Techniques on page 11. Machine stitch and cut for sleeves and square neck. Sew or graft the shoulders together. Using smaller needle and Color 1, pick up sts around the neck from the right side. Knit 3 rnds, decreasing 1 st in each corner every rnd. Purl 1 rnd. Knit 5 rnds for facing, increasing 1 st in each corner. Bind off. Sew in the sleeves. Weave all loose ends into the back of the fabric and sew the facings to the wrong side.

Pants: Using smaller needle and Color 1, cast on 48 (52) 56 sts. Join, being careful not to twist sts. Knit 7 rnds for facing, purl 1 rnd, and knit 6 rnds. Change to larger needles and Color 2. Make the first st on the rnd the marking st, and work this st in Color 2 every rnd. Knit 1 rnd. On the next rnd, inc evenly spaced to 96 (104) 112 sts. Work Border 2 until the leg measures 10¼" (11¾") 13⅜" from the purl rnd. Bind off the first 5 sts on the rnd (including the marking st). Continue to knit around until 4 sts remain. Bind off these 4 sts. Make the other leg the same. Put the sts from both legs onto larger circular needle. Cast on 1 st at both center front and center back (where the two parts meet). These 2 sts are marking sts; work them in Color 2 every rnd and make the decs on each side of them—176 (192) 208 sts. Work the design as you dec 1 st on each side of the marking sts every 4th rnd 6 times—152 (168) 184 sts remain. Then dec 1 st on each side of the center back marking st only every 8th rnd 3 times—146 (162) 178 sts remain. When the pants measure 8⅝" (9¾") 11" from the crotch, change to smaller needle and finish

using Color 2 only. On the first rnd, dec 6 (14) 24 sts evenly spaced—140 (148) 154 sts remain. Knit 6 rnds, purl 1 rnd, and knit 7 rnds. Bind off.

Finishing: Sew the facings to the wrong side leaving a small opening at the waist for elastic. Sew the crotch seam.

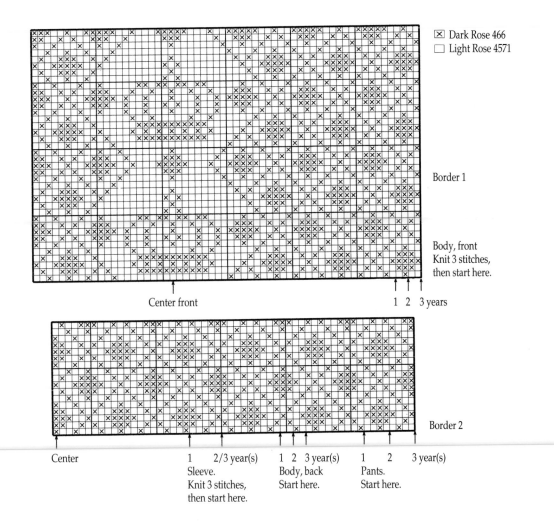

☒ Dark Rose 466
☐ Light Rose 4571

Border 1

Body, front
Knit 3 stitches,
then start here.

Center front

1 2 3 years

Border 2

Center

1   2/3 year(s)
Sleeve.
Knit 3 stitches,
then start here.

1 2 3 year(s)
Body, back
Start here.

1   2   3 year(s)
Pants.
Start here.

MODEL 8

Princess Suit for Big Girls

Sizes: 6 (9) 12 years

Finished Measurements:

Chest 29⅞" (33") 37"

Length, pullover 16⅛" (18⅛") 20⅞"

Waist, skirt 22" (24") 25"

Length, skirt 11¾" (13¾") 15¾"

Yarn: Rauma Finullgarn

Colorway 1

Color 1: Old Rose #427

Pullover and skirt: 50 (50) 50g

Color 2: Light Rose #4571

Pullover and skirt: 150 (200) 250g

Color 3: Dark Rose #466

Pullover: 200 (250) 300g

Skirt: 150 (200) 250g

Colorway 2

Color 1: Clear Blue #437

Color 2: Light Green #493

Color 3: Green #421

Gauge: 27 sts and 32 rows over pattern = 4 ×
4 inches. Make a swatch to assure proper
gauge.

Needle suggestion: Double-point and circular needles sizes 2 and 3 (2.5mm and
3mm), or size to obtain gauge.

Body: Using smaller needle and Color 1,
cast on 176 (192) 216 sts. Join, being careful
not to twist sts. Knit 7 rnds for facing, purl 1
rnd, and knit 6 rnds. Change to Color 2. Knit
1 rnd and change to larger needle. Make 3
marking sts on each side. Knit the marking

sts in Color 3 every rnd, and make the incs
on each side of them. Work Border 1 on the
front, and Border 2 on the back. Inc 1 st on
each side of the marking sts (4 sts every rnd),
counting from where you started Color 2, as
follows: Size 6 years: Inc 4 sts after the 6th
rnd, then every 6th rnd 7 times for a total of
208 sts. Size 9 years: Inc 4 sts after the 7th
rnd, then every 6th rnd 6 times, and every
7th rnd 2 times for a total of 228 sts. Size 12
years: Inc 4 sts every 7th rnd 9 times for a
total of 256 sts. Work the design until the
body measures 6¾" (7⅞") 9⅜" from the
purl rnd. Bind off the marking sts. On the
next rnd, cast on 2 new sts over the bound-
off sts, and purl the new sts every rnd using
both strands. They will be machine stitched
and cut later on. Work until the body measures 14" (15¾") 18⅛" from the purl rnd.
Shape for square neck by binding off center
front 31 (31) 35 sts. On the next rnd, cast on 2
sts over bound-off sts. Purl the new sts every
rnd using both strands. They will be ma-

chine stitched and cut later on. When the
body measures 15⅜" (17¼") 20", bind off
center back 31 (31) 35 sts for back neck. On
the next rnd, cast on 2 sts over the bound-off
sts. Purl the new sts every rnd using both
strands. Work until the body measures full
length. Put all the sts on a holder, or bind off.

Sleeves: Make 2. Using smaller needles
and Color 1, cast on 60 (66) 68 sts. Join, being
careful not to twist sts. Knit 7 rnds for facing,
purl 1 rnd, and knit 7 rnds. Using Color 2,
knit 1 rnd. Make 3 marking sts at the underarm center. They are worked in Color 3
every rnd, and the incs take place on each
side of them. Change to larger needles and
work Border 2. Start increasing after the 4th
rnd as follows: Size 6 years: Inc 2 sts every
3rd rnd 34 times. Size 9 years: Inc 2 sts every
3rd rnd 34 times, then every 4th rnd 4 times.
Size 12 years: Inc 2 sts every 3rd rnd 39
times, then every 4th rnd 6 times. Change to
Color 1 when the sleeve measures 13⅜"
(15⅜") 18⅛". Knit 3 rnds, purl 1 rnd, and

knit 7 rnds for facing. Bind off.

Finishing: For details on finishing, see Knitting Techniques on page 11. Machine stitch and cut for sleeves and square neck. Sew or graft the shoulders together. Using smaller needle and Color 1, pick up sts around the neck from the right side. Knit 3 rnds, decreasing 1 st at each corner every rnd. Purl 1 rnd. Knit 5 rnds, increasing 1 st at each corner every rnd. Sew in the sleeves. Weave all loose ends into the back of the fabric, and sew the facings to the wrong side.

Skirt: The skirt is worked in stockinette st from the bottom up. Using smaller needle and Color 1, cast on 328 (384) 432 sts. Join, being careful not to twist sts. Knit 4 rnds, purl 1 rnd, and knit 3 rnds. Change to Color 2, and knit 2 rnds. Finish the skirt using Color 3. Place 4 markers with 82 (96) 108 sts between markers (sections). Make the 2 first sts in each section the marking sts. Dec 1 st on each side of the marking sts—8 sts each rnd—as follows: Size 6 years: Dec 8 sts every other rnd 5 times, then every 3rd rnd 11 times, every 11th rnd 4 times, and every 15th rnd once only. Size 9 years: Dec 8 sts every 3rd rnd 19 times, then every 8th rnd 3 times, every 7th rnd 3 times, and every 15th rnd once. Size 12 years: Dec 8 sts every 3rd rnd 24 times, every 8th rnd 5 times, every 7th rnd once, and every 15th rnd once. Knit 6 rnds, purl 1 rnd, and knit 7 rnds. Bind off.

Finishing: Sew the casing to the wrong side, leaving a small opening at the waist for elastic.

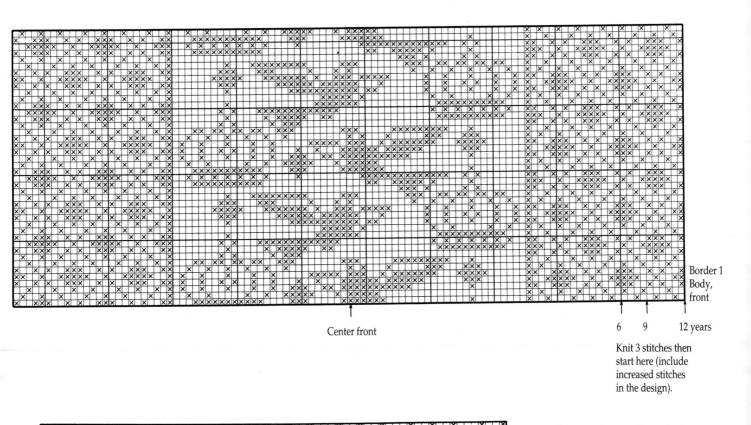

Center front

6 9 12 years

Knit 3 stitches then
start here (include
increased stitches
in the design).

Border 1
Body,
front

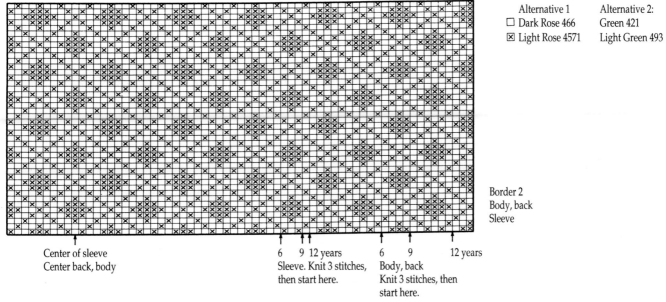

Alternative 1
☐ Dark Rose 466
☒ Light Rose 4571

Alternative 2:
Green 421
Light Green 493

Border 2
Body, back
Sleeve

Center of sleeve
Center back, body

6 9 12 years
Sleeve. Knit 3 stitches,
then start here.

6 9 12 years
Body, back
Knit 3 stitches, then
start here.

MODEL 9

I Want a Small Dog

Sizes: 8 (10) 12 years

Finished Measurements:

Chest: 32¼" (35⅜") 37"

Length: 17¾" (18⅞") 21¼"

Head circumference: 18½" (18½") 20⅜"

Yarn: Rauma Finullgarn

Medium Green #430; 150 (150) 200g

Light Green #493; 150 (150) 200g

Charcoal #4387; 300 (300) 400g

Orange Rust #419; 50 (50) 50g

Red Rust #428; 50 (50) 50g

Burgundy #497; 50 (50) 50g

Gauge: 27 sts and 32 rows over pattern = 4 × 4 inches. Make a swatch to assure proper gauge.

Needle suggestion: Double-point and circular needles sizes 2 and 3 (2.5mm and 3mm), or size to obtain gauge.

Body: Using smaller needle and Burgundy, cast on 196 (210) 224 sts. Join, being careful not to twist sts. Knit facing for 1½", purl 1 rnd, and knit 1 rnd. Work Border 1. Change to larger needle and inc evenly spaced to 224 (242) 256 sts. Work Border 2 with dogs at center front and center back, and stripes on the sides. One dog repeat goes over 71 sts, and there are 41 (50) 57 sts for stripes on each side. Work the

changes in background colors as indicated on the chart. Work until the body measures 14⅛" (15⅜") 17¾". Bind off center front 36 (38) 38 sts for neck opening. On the next rnd, cast on 3 sts over the bound-off sts. Purl the new sts every rnd using both strands. They will be machine stitched and cut later on. Work in the rnd for 2¼" (2¾") 2¾". Bind off center back 36 (38) 38 sts for back neck opening. Now work stockinette stitch back and forth for 3/4". Put remaining sts on a holder, or bind off.

Sleeves: Make 2. Using smaller needles and Burgundy, cast on 41 (43) 45 sts. Join, being careful not to twist sts. Work the facing as the body, then Border 1. Change to

larger needles, increasing evenly spaced to 55 (59) 63 sts. Work stripes as on the sides of the body. *At the same time,* inc 2 sts at underarm every 3rd rnd until 125 (135) 145 sts. Work until the sleeve measures 15⅜" (16⅞") 18½" from the purl rnd. Using Charcoal, knit 8 rnds for facing, increasing 2 sts at underarm every rnd. Bind off.

Finishing: For details on finishing, see Finishing Techniques on page 11. Machine stitch and cut for sleeves and square neck. Graft or sew the shoulders together. Using Charcoal, pick up sts around the neck. Using Burgundy, knit 2 rnds and purl 1 rnd. Knit 6 rnds, increasing 2 sts at each corner every rnd. Bind off. Sew in the sleeves. Weave all loose ends into the back of the fabric and sew the facings to the wrong side. Steam lightly.

Hat: 8/10 (12) years. Check your gauge. A small difference in gauge can make a big difference in the finished size. Using smaller needle and Burgundy, cast on 126 (140) sts. Join, being careful not to twist sts. Knit the facing and Border 1 as for the body. Change to larger needle and inc 2 (0) sts evenly spaced. Make the 32nd, 64th, 96th, and 128th (35th, 70th, 105th, and 140th) sts marking sts. Work them in Charcoal, and do the increasing—8 sts each rnd—on each side them. Work the stripe design as the sides of the body, and *at the same time,* inc every rnd for 22 rnds. Using Charcoal, knit 1 rnd and purl 1 rnd. Now dec 1 st on each side of the 4 marking sts every rnd until 8 sts remain. Put remaining sts on yarn, gather, and fasten off. Steam lightly. Using the Red colors, make a small pompom and sew to the top.

■ Charcoal 4387
   Color changes:
▣ Orange Rust 419/Red Rust 428
□ Medium Green 430/Light Green 493

Changes in background colors

430

493

430

493

430

493

430

419

428

419

Border 2

Border 1

Center front
Center back

Most children love animals, but not all of them are lucky enough
to have a farm in the neighborhood, or a cat in the kitchen.
If mom and dad aren't open to having chickens in the yard,
goldfish in the tub, or a horse in the garage, perhaps a sweater with an
animal design will do. Here are several to choose from.

Suit with Birds

Sizes: 1/2 (1) 2 years
Finished Measurements:
    Chest: 24⅜" (33") 38½"
    Length: 20⅞" (25⅝") 27¼"
Yarn: Rauma Babygarn
    Natural #B11; 200 (250) 300g
    Light Blue #B51; 200 (200) 250g
    Medium Blue #B67; 50 (50) 50g
Gauge: 32 sts and 36 rows over pattern = 4 ×
    4 inches. Make a swatch to assure proper
    gauge.
Needle suggestion: Double-point and circu-
    lar needles sizes 0 and 2 (2mm and
    2.5mm), or size to obtain gauge.

Legs: Make 2. Using smaller needle and
Medium Blue, cast on 48 (48) 50 sts. Join,
being careful not to twist sts. Work k1
through the back loop, p1 ribbing for 1½".
Change to larger needles and inc evenly
spaced to 79 (89) 99 sts. Work Border 1,
increasing 2 sts on the inside of the leg every
3rd rnd. Work Border 2, and continue inc
until 123 (143) 162 sts are on the needles, and
the leg measures 9" (10¼") 11". Now dec for
the crotch. Work back and forth, decreasing
on each side (at the inseam) as follows: Dec 2
sts every other row 6 (7) 8 times each side.

Body: Put the sts from both legs onto one
circular needle. The 4 center front sts are
marking sts. Purl the marking sts every rnd

using both strands. They will be machine stitched and cut later on. Dec to make the design come out even at the center of the back. Work the bird repeat of Border 3 on each side of the center front purl sts. Work until the suit measures 20" (22¾") 24¾", and put the sts with the bird repeat on a holder. Now work back and forth for 1⅛". Bind off center back 28 sts. Work for 3/4" and bind off.

Sleeves: Make 2. Using smaller needles and Medium Blue, cast on 28 (32) 32 sts. Join, being careful not to twist sts. Work ribbing as for body for 1½". Change to larger needles and inc evenly spaced to 49 (51) 57 sts. Start Border 1, and *at the same time* inc 2 sts at underarm every other rnd. After Border 1, work Border 2. Inc to 95 (109) 129 sts. Work until the sleeve measures 5½" (8⅝") 10⅝". Purl 6 rnds for facing, increasing 2 sts at underarm every rnd.

Finishing: For details on finishing, see Finishing Techniques on page 11. Machine stitch and cut open for sleeves. Sew the shoulders together. Put the sts from the holder on a needle and pick up sts around the neck for the hood. Work birds on each side of the center front purl sts and the diamond shapes on the back. Work until the hood measures 7½" (7⅞") 8¼". Bind off the purl sts, and on the next rnd, cast on 19 sts over the bound-off sts. Work the bird repeat on the front and the diamonds on the back. After the bird repeat, work the diamonds all the way around. You may not be at the right place in the diamond pattern to get a smooth transition as on the chart. Therefore, the transition will look different from knitter to knitter. You may "cheat" a little if you think it does not look right. For example, you may add 1 st to the bird repeat, or maybe knit 1

rnd less. At this point, start decreasing. Dec 2 sts on each side every 3rd rnd. It may be a good idea to make 1 st on each side of the hood a marking st, working the marking sts in the center front always in the same color, and decreasing on each side of them. Work until 4 sts remain. Put remaining sts on yarn, gather, and fasten off. **Facings:** Machine stitch along the purl sts at center front of the body and cut open. Using Medium Blue, pick up sts along both fronts in one piece. Knit 1 row from the right side, knit 1 row from the wrong side, then work stockinette stitch for 8 rows, increasing 2 sts on both sides of the lower corners (by the crotch), and 2 sts on each side at the neck opening. Bind off. Sew on clasps. Sew in the sleeves. Sew the crotch seam, weave all loose ends into the back of the fabric, and sew the

facings to the wrong side. Steam lightly. Using Medium Blue, make a pompom and sew to the top of the hood.

☐ Natural B11

■ Light Blue B51

⊙ Purl Stitches

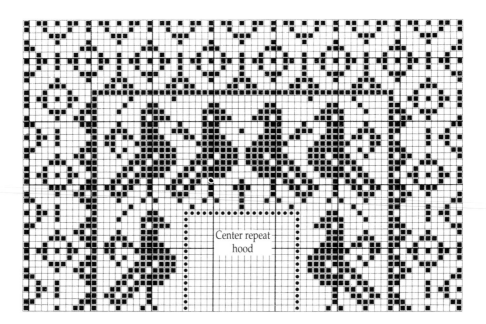

Center repeat
hood

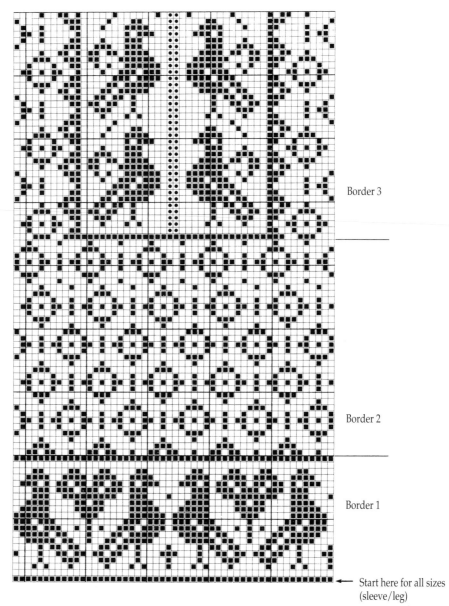

Border 3

Border 2

Border 1

← Start here for all sizes
(sleeve/leg)

Squirrel Suit for Baby

Sizes: 3 (6) 12 months

Finished Measurements:

    Chest: 25¼" (27¼") 29⅛"

    Length: 11⅛" (11¾") 12¼"

Yarn: Røros Lamullgarn

    Natural #L11; 50 (50) 100g

    Red #L43; 100 (100) 100g

    Blue #L65; 50 (50) 50g

    Rose #L47; 50 (50) 50g

    Dark Blue #L82; 50 (50) 50g

You do not need much Blue, Rose, or Dark Blue, so if you have leftovers in these colors, use them first.

Gauge: 29 sts and 33 rows over pattern = 4 × 4 inches. Make a swatch to assure proper gauge.

Needle suggestion: Double-point and circular needles size 0 and 2 (2mm and 2.5mm), and a long circular size 1 (2mm) for the edging, or size to obtain gauge.

Body: Work in the rnd and cut the front open. The cardigan has a double-breasted closing. Using larger needle and Red, cast on 246 (265) 284 sts. Join, being careful not to twist sts. Knit 1 rnd and purl 1 rnd. The first and the last st in the rnd are front marking sts. Purl the marking sts every rnd using two strands. The next 74 (80) 86 sts are the left front. Make the next st a marking st (side), and knit it in Natural throughout Border 1, and in Blue throughout Border 2. The next 93

Squirrel Pullover for Baby

Sizes: 3 (6) 12 months

Finished Measurements:

    Chest: 25¼" (27¼") 29⅛"

    Length: 11¼" (11¾") 12¼"

Yarn: Røros Lamullgarn

    Natural #L11 50 (50) 100g

    Red #L43; 100 (100) 100g

    Blue #L65; 50 (50) 50g

    Rose #L47; 50 (50) 50g

    Dark Blue #L82; 50 (50) 50g

You do not need much Blue, Rose, or Dark Blue, so if you have leftovers in these colors, use them first.

Gauge: 29 sts and 33 rows over pattern = 4 × 4 inches. Make a swatch to assure proper gauge.

Needle suggestion: Double-point and circular needles sizes 0 and 1 (2mm and 2.5mm), or size to obtain gauge.

Body: Using Dark Blue and smaller needle, cast on 188 (204) 216 sts. Join, being careful not to twist sts. Knit 7 rnds for facing, purl 1 rnd, knit 4 rnds. Change to larger needle. Using Red, knit 1 rnd. Make the first st on the rnd the marking st for the right side. The next 93 (101) 107 sts are for the front, and the next st is the marking st for the left side. The marking sts are worked in Natural through Border 1, and in Blue through Border 2. The back goes over 93 (101) 107 sts. Work Border 1 according to the chart. The arrows indicate where to start the

(101) 107 sts are the back. Make the next st a marking st (side), and work it as the previous marking st. Remaining sts are the right front. Work Border 1. The arrows on the chart indicate where in the design to start the different parts. B1–B2 are left front, C1–C2 are the back, and A1–A2 are the right front. Work Border 1 for 41 (34) 39 rnds, and start shaping for the diagonal closing at the center front. Dec 1 st every rnd on each side of the purl sts 32 (27) 36 times, then every other rnd 10 (18) 14 times, and *at the same time* work Border 1 until the body measures 9⅜" (10") 10⅝". Continue the shaping, but work Border 2 according to the chart. After finishing Border 2, the body measures approximately 11¼" (11¾") 12¼". Bind off remaining sts, or put them on holders if you choose to graft the shoulders together.

Sleeves: Make 2. Using Dark Blue and smaller needles, cast on 52 (54) 56 sts. Join, being careful not to twist sts. Knit 7 rnds for facing, then purl 1 rnd and knit 4 rnds. Change to larger needles and knit 1 rnd using Red. Work Border 1. The arrows on the chart (D1-D2) indicate where the sleeve design starts and ends. Make the first st on the rnd the marking st. This st is worked in Natural, and the incs take place on each side of it. After 6 (5) 5 rnds of design, start the incs as follows: Size 3 months: Inc 2 sts every 5th rnd 3 times, then 2 sts every 6th rnd 6 times (70 sts). Size 6 months: Inc 2 sts every 4th rnd 8 times, then 2 sts every 5th rnd 4 times (78 sts). Size 12 months: Inc 2 sts every 4th rnd 10 times, then 2 sts every 5th rnd 2 times (80 sts). Work until the sleeve mea-

sures 6¼" (6⅝") 7". Change to Dark Blue and finish with knit 3 rnds, purl 1 rnd, then knit 7 rnds for facing. Bind off.

Finishing: For details on finishing, see Knitting Techniques on page 11. Machine stitch and cut open for sleeve openings and neck opening. Sew or graft the shoulders together. The neck edge, the front edges, and the lower edge are worked in one piece. Using a size 1 (2mm) long circular needle, Dark Blue, and working from the right side, pick up sts around the neck, along the front edges, and around the lower edge. Pick up the st inside the machine seams in the front and around the neck, and inside the purl rnd along the lower edge. Knit 4 rnds, increasing 1 st every rnd at the lower corner of each front band, and every other rnd at the top corner of the front bands. Purl 1 rnd, then knit 7 rnds for facing, decreasing 1 st every rnd at the lower corners of the front bands, and every other rnd at the top corners. This will make the facing lay flat. Sew the facings to the wrong side. Sew in the sleeves. Weave all loose ends into the back of the fabric. Cords to tie: Using Dark Blue, twist four 10" long strands. Sew one cord to each top corner on the front, one on the wrong side the same height by the marking st, and one on the right side the same height as the corner. Now the cardigan can be tied, first on the inside, then on the outside. Alternative to twisted cords: Using crochet hook, pull a loop through at the above described place for the cords. Make chain sts for 10", turn, and do 1 single crochet in each chain st going back. Finish off.

design for the different parts. C1–C2 make the front and the back on the pullover. Work Border 1 until the body measures 9⅜" (10") 10⅝", then work Border 2. After finishing Border 2, the body measures approximately 11¼" (11¾") 12¼". Using Dark Blue, purl 1 rnd, then knit 7 rnds for facing. Put remaining sts on holders if you want to graft the shoulders together, or bind off if you want to sew them together.

Sleeves: Make 2. Using Dark Blue and smaller needles, cast on 52 (54) 56 sts. Join, being careful not to twist sts. Knit 7 rnds for facing, purl 1 rnd, and knit 4 rnds. Change to larger needles. Using Red knit 1 rnd. Start Border 1. The arrows on the chart (D1–D2) indicate where the sleeve design starts and ends. Make the first st on the rnd the marking st. Work this st in Natural every rnd, and inc on each side of this st. Start increasing after 6 (5) 5 rnds of design as follows: Size 3 months: Inc 2 sts every 5th rnd 3 times, then 2 sts every 6th rnd 6 times (70 sts). Size 6 months: Inc 2 sts every 4th rnd 8 times, then 2 sts every 5th rnd 4 times (78 sts). Size 12 months: Inc 2 sts every 4th rnd 10 times, then 2 sts every 5th rnd 2 times (80 sts). When the sleeve measures 6¼" (6⅝") 7", finish off in Dark Blue knitting 3 rnds, purling 1 rnd, and knitting 7 rnds for facing. Bind off.

Finishing: For details on finishing, see Knitting Techniques on page 11. Machine stitch and cut open for sleeve openings. Fold the neck facing and sew to the wrong side. The neck opening is 5½" (5¾") 6" wide. Sew or graft the shoulders together. Sew in the sleeves. Weave all loose ends into the back of the fabric and sew the facings to the wrong side.

Border 2

Border 1

12   6   3 months
B2 and C2 end here
Cardigan: Left front back
Pullover: Front back

12   6   3 months
A2 ends here
Cardigan: Right front

12-6-3 months
D2 ends here
Sleeve

Center front/Center back, pullover
Center back, cardigan
Center of sleeve

3-6-12

3   6   12 months
B1 Starts here
Cardigan: Left front

3   6   12 months
A1 and C1 Start here
Cardigan: Right front, back
Pullover: Front, back

☐ Natural L11
☒ Red L43
• Blue L65
▼ Rose L47
■ Dark Blue L82

MODEL 12

Squirrel Cardigan

Sizes: 2 (4) 6 years

Finished Measurements:

Chest: 25¼" (27½") 29⅞"

Hips: 23¼" (25⅝") 27½"

Length: 10¼" (11⅜") 12½"

Yarn: Røros Lamullgarn

Dark Green #L63; 50 (50) 50g

Natural #L11; 100 (100) 150g

Dark Blue #L82; 100 (150) 150g

Green #L94; 50 (50) 50g

Rose #L47; 50 (50) 50g

Gauge: 29 sts and 33 rows over pattern = 4 × 4 inches. Make a swatch to assure proper gauge.

Needle suggestion: Double-point and circular needles sizes 0 and 2 (2mm and 2.5mm). Long circular needle size 0 (2mm) for the edges, or size to obtain gauge.

Body: The body is made in the rnd and later cut open for sleeves and front. Using Dark Blue and larger needle, cast on 170 (190) 203 sts. Join, being careful not to twist sts. Knit 1 rnd and purl 1 rnd. Knit the next rnd, increasing evenly spaced to 189 (209) 225 sts. The first and the last st on the rnd are marking sts for center front, and are purled every rnd using two strands. They are for machine stitching and cutting later on. The next 46 (51) 55 sts make the right front. The next st is side marking st, and is knit in

Natural through Border 1, and in the Greens through Border 2. The next 93 (103) 111 sts are the sts for the back. The following st is the left side marking st, and it is worked as the first side marking st. Remaining sts make the left front. Work Border 1. Start as indicated by the arrows on the chart. When the body measures 8½" (9¼") 10¾", start Border 2, and start shaping the square neck. Using Dark Blue, knit 1 rnd, binding off center front 42 (44) 48 sts, including the 2 purl sts at center front. On the next rnd, cast on 2 sts over the bound-off sts. Purl the 2 new sts every rnd using two strands. After 8 rnds of Border 2, bind off center back 41 (43) 47 sts for the back neck opening. On the next rnd, cast on 2 sts over the bound-off sts. Purl the 2 new sts every rnd using two strands. After finishing Border 2, the body measures full length. Using Dark Green, knit 1 rnd. If you prefer to graft the shoulders together, put remaining sts on holders. Bind off if you want to sew the shoulders together.

Sleeves: Make 2. Using Dark Green and smaller needles, cast on 53 (56) 56 sts. Join, being careful not to twist sts. Knit 7 rnds for facing, purl 1 rnd, and knit 4 rnds. Change to larger needles and inc evenly spaced to 66 (70) 70 sts. Work Border 1. The first st on the rnd is a marking st, and it is worked in Natural through Border 1, and in Greens through Border 2. Inc on each side of the marking st. After 6 (7) 6 rnds of Border 1, inc as follows: Size 2 years: Inc 2 sts every 5th rnd 7 times, then 2 sts every 6th rnd 3 times (86 sts). Size 4 years: Inc 2 sts every 6th rnd 6 times, then 2 sts every 7th rnd 5 times (92 sts). Size 6 years: Inc 2 sts every 6th rnd 14 times (98 sts). When the sleeve measures 7" (9") 10⅝", start Border 2 by knitting 1 rnd Dark Blue. Finish using Dark Green knitting

1 rnd, purling 1 rnd, then knitting 7 rnds for facing. Bind off.

Finishing: For details on finishing, see Knitting Techniques on page 11. Machine stitch and cut for sleeve openings, square neck, and center front opening. Sew or graft the shoulders together. Work the edge all around the cardigan in one piece. Using Dark Green and a long size 2mm needle, right side facing, pick up the sts around the neck, along the front edges, and along the lower edge. Pick up sts in the row inside the machine seams at center front and around the neck, and inside the purl rnd at the lower edge. Knit 4 rnds, decreasing 1 st every rnd at each corner of the neck opening, and increasing 1 st at the upper and lower front corners. Purl 1 rnd, then knit 7 rnds for facing, decreasing as earlier increased, and increasing as earlier decreased, to make the facing lay flat. Weave all loose ends into the back of the fabric, and sew the facings to the wrong side. Optional: Sew 3 (4) 4 clasps to the front. The cardigan is nice without clasps also.

M O D E L   1 2

Neck opening
front and back
6 4 2 years

Neck opening
front and back
2 4 6 years

Border 2

Border 1

6   4   2 years
Right front and back
End here

4/6 2 years
Sleeve
Ends here

Right front
Start here

Left front
End here

2 4/6 years
Sleeve
Start here.

2   4   6 years
Left front and back.
Start here.

Center back

- ⊡ Dark Green L63
- ☐ Natural L11
- ☒ Dark Blue L82
- ⦿ Green L94
- ⊡ Rosy Red L47

MODEL 13

Bird Song

Sizes: 6 (8) 10 (12) 14 years

Finished Measurements:

Chest: 31½" (33⅞") 36¼" (37") 38½"

Length: 16⅛" (17¼") 18⅞" (21¼") 23⅝"

Head circumference: 20⅜" (20⅜") 22⅜" (22⅜") 22⅜"

Yarn: Rauma Finullgarn

Pale Yellow #402; 150 (150) 200 (200) 200g

Charcoal #4387; 300 (300) 300 (350) 350g

Light Rust #434; 50 (50) 50 (50) 50g

Dark Rust #419; 50 (50) 50 (50) 50g

Green #430; 50 (50) 50 (50) 50g

Gauge: 27 sts and 32 rows over pattern = 4 × 4 inches. Make a swatch to assure proper gauge.

Needle suggestions: Double-point and circular needles sizes 2 and 3 (2.5mm and 3mm), or size to obtain gauge.

Body: Using Green and smaller needle, cast on 180 (192) 204 (228) 240 sts. Join, being careful not to twist sts. Knit 1½" in the rnd for facing, purl 1 rnd, then knit 2 rnds. Work Border 1. Change to larger needle and inc evenly spaced to 218 (230) 248 (254) 266 sts. Work Border 2 according to the chart. The pullover has birds on the front and on the back. Two sts, one on each side, are marking sts, and are worked in Charcoal. Sizes 6 and 8 years have 6 birds in the first row; sizes 10, 12, and 14 years have 8 birds. Work birds and zigzag design until the body measures 13" (14⅛") 15⅜" (17¾") 20" from the purl rnd. Bind off center front 36 (36) 38 (38) 40 rnd. Bind off center front 36 (36) 38 (38) 40

sts for front neck. On the next rnd, cast on 2 sts over bound-off sts. Purl the 2 new sts every rnd using two strands. They are for machine stitching and cutting later on. Continue working in the rnd. Work until the body measures 15⅜" (16½") 18⅛" (20⅜") 22¾". Bind off center back 36 (36) 38 (38) 40 sts for back neck. Work back and forth for 3/4". Bind off or put remaining sts on holders.

Sleeves: Make 2. Using Green and smaller needles, cast on 36 (48) 48 (48) 48 sts. Join, being careful not to twist sts. Work facing and lower border as the body. Change to larger needles and inc evenly spaced to 43 (51) 53 (55) 57 sts. Work zigzag design, and *at the same time* inc 2 sts at underarm every 3rd rnd to 119 (129) 145 (157) 163 sts. Work until the sleeve measures 13¾" (15⅜") 16⅞" (18½") 20". Purl 8 rnds for facing, increasing 2 sts at underarm every rnd. Bind off.

Finishing: For details on finishing, see Knitting Techniques on page 11. Machine stitch and cut for sleeve openings. Sew or graft the shoulders together. Using Charcoal, pick up sts around the neck. Using Green, knit 2 rnds and purl 1 rnd. Then knit 8 rnds, increasing 2 sts at each corner every rnd. Bind off. Sew in the sleeves. Weave all loose ends into the back of the fabric, and sew the facings to the wrong side. Using duplicate st, embroider the details on the flowers. Steam lightly.

Hat: 6/8 (10/12/14) years. Check your gauge. A small change in gauge can make a big difference in the finished size. Using Green and larger needle, cast on 140 (154) sts. Join, being careful not to twist sts. Knit in the rnd for 3⅛", purl 1 rnd, knit 1 rnd. Work the bird border from the hat chart. All the

birds face the same direction. Using Charcoal, purl 2 rnds according to the chart decreasing (increasing) evenly spaced to 138 (156) sts. Work the zigzag design, and *at the same time* dec according to the chart on each side of the two Charcoal sts. The hat has 6 sections. Work and dec until only Charcoal sts remain. Put remaining sts on yarn and gather. Make a small Green pompom and sew to the top of the hat. Weave all loose ends into the back of the fabric and sew the facing to the wrong side. Steam lightly.

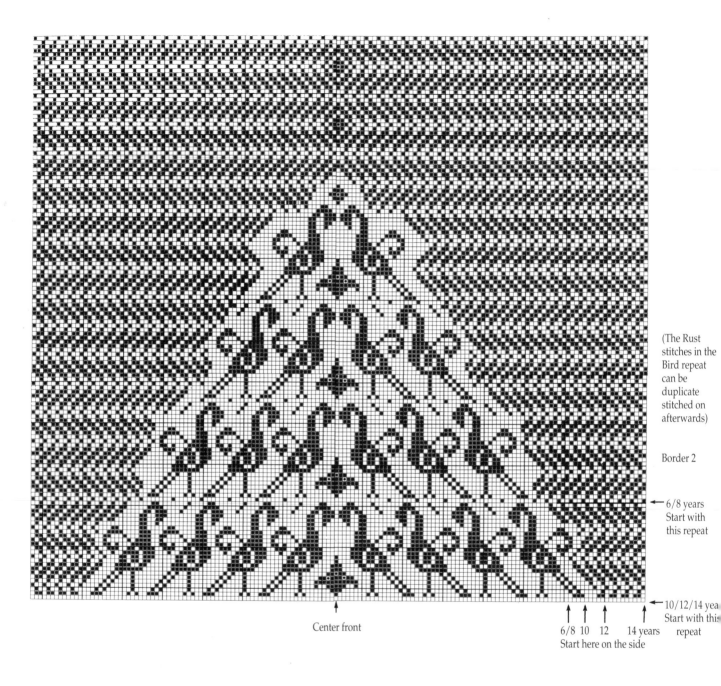

(The Rust
stitches in the
Bird repeat
can be
duplicate
stitched on
afterwards)

Border 2

← 6/8 years
Start with
this repeat

← 10/12/14 yea
Start with this
repeat

Center front

6/8 10 12   14 years
Start here on the side

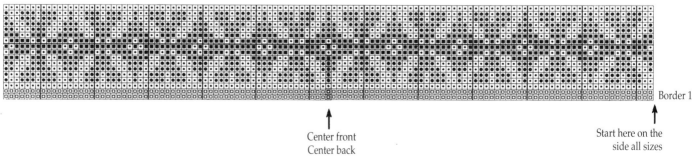

Border 1

Center front
Center back

Start here on the
side all sizes

Mittens: 6/8 (10/12/14) years. Using Green and smaller needles, cast on 40 (42) sts. Join, being careful not to twist sts. Work k1, p1 ribbing as follows: Green 2 rnds, Dark Rust 2 rnds, Light Rust 1 rnd, then Charcoal until the ribbing measures 2". Change to larger needles, increasing evenly spaced to 46 (50) sts. Work the design, and inc for the thumb according to the chart. At X, put 9 sts on a holder for thumb opening. On the next rnd, cast on 9 sts over the sts on the holder. Continue working and decreasing according to the chart. Dec as follows: At the beginning of the 1st and the 3rd needle, sl 1, k1, psso; at the end of the 2nd and the 4th needle, k2tog. Knit and dec until 8 sts remain. Put remaining sts on yarn and gather. Fasten off.

Thumb: Slip the sts from the holder onto a needle and pick up 9 (11) sts along the cast-on sts, plus 1 st on each side, totaling 20 (22) sts. Work and dec according to the thumb chart. Make the other mitten, reversing shaping.

■ Charcoal 4387

□ Pale yellow 402

▣ Green 430

◉ Light Rust 434

■ Dark Rust 419

⊡ Charcoal 4387

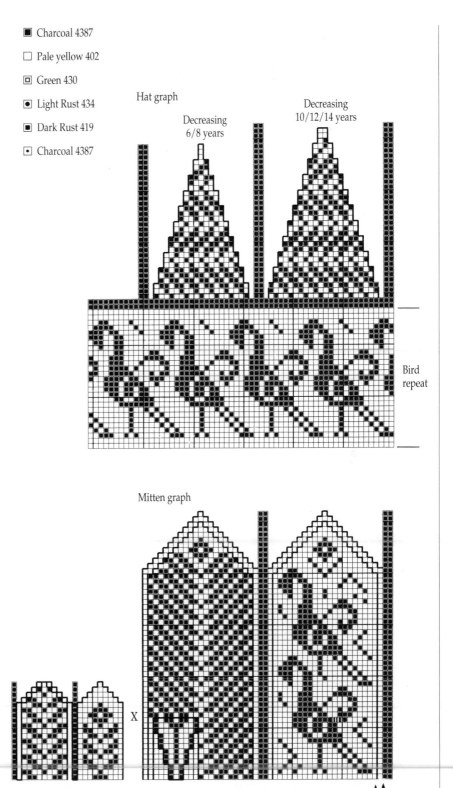

Hat graph

Decreasing 6/8 years

Decreasing 10/12/14 years

Bird repeat

Mitten graph

Thumb

X

6/8 years
10/12/14 years
Start here

MODEL 14

Stella

Sizes: 6 (8) 10 years

Finished Measurements:

Chest: 31½" (33") 34⅝"

Length: 17¾" (18⅞") 20⅜"

Head circumference: 19¼" (20⅜") 20⅜"

Yarn: Rauma Finullgarn

Light Green #493; 200 (250) 300g

Dark Green #485; 50 (100) 100g

Red #439; 250 (300) 350g

Turquoise #483; 50 (50) 50g

Yellow #450; 50 (50) 50g

Gauge: 27 sts and 32 rows over pattern = 4 × 4 inches. Make a swatch to assure proper gauge.

Needle suggestion: Double-point and circular needles sizes 2 and 3 (2.5mm and 3mm), or size to obtain gauge.

Body: Using Dark Green and smaller needle, cast on 180 (190) 200 sts. Join, being careful not to twist sts. Work k1, p1 ribbing for 2 rnds. Change to Red and continue ribbing until the ribbing measures 2". Change to larger needle, increasing evenly spaced to 216 (228) 240 sts. Work Border 1 according to the chart until the body measures 8⅝" (9¾") 11⅜". Work Borders 2 and 3. Shape for front and back neck according to the chart, working back and forth. Bind off and dec for front neck according to the chart. Work back and forth. Bind off and dec for the back neck according to the chart. Finish each side separately, working back and forth. After finishing the chart, put remaining sts on holders, or bind off.

Sleeves: Make 2. Using Dark Green and smaller needles, cast on 42 (44) 44 sts. Join, being careful not to twist sts. Work ribbing as for body. Change to larger needles, increasing evenly spaced to 47 (51) 53 sts. Work Border 1, and *at the same time* inc 2 sts at underarm every 3rd rnd to 119 (125) 135 sts. Work until the sleeve measures 13¾" (15⅜") 16⅞". Work Border 2. Purl 8 rnds for facing, increasing 2 sts at underarm every rnd. Bind off.

Finishing: For details on finishing, see Knitting Techniques on page 11. Machine stitch and cut for sleeve openings. Sew or graft the shoulders together. Using Red and larger needle, pick up sts around the neck. Start at the left front corner, work across the back neck, and finish at the right front corner. Work k1 through the back loop, p1 ribbing back and forth for 13 rows. Finish off using Dark Green for 2 rows and bind off. Sew the sides of the neck band along the front of the neck opening. The sides overlap.

Hat: 6 (8–10) years. Check your gauge. A small difference in gauge can make a big difference in the finished size. Using Red and smaller needles, cast on 132 (144) sts. Join, being careful not to twist sts. Knit facing for 2", then purl 1 rnd. Work Border 2, then Border 1 using the same colors as for the body. Break the yarn when the hat measures 7" from the purl rnd. Put remaining sts on yarn and gather.

Ear flaps: Using Red, pick up 20 sts on the inside of the hat. Turn, and pick up another 20 sts on the outside, making a double ear flap. Knit in the rnd until the ear flap measures 3/4". Now dec 2 sts on each side (1 st on each side of a center st) every rnd until 4 sts remain. Put remaining sts on yarn. Fasten off. Make the other ear flap. Make a Dark Green pompom and sew to the top of the hat. Weave all loose ends into the back of the fabric, sew the facing to the wrong side, and steam lightly.

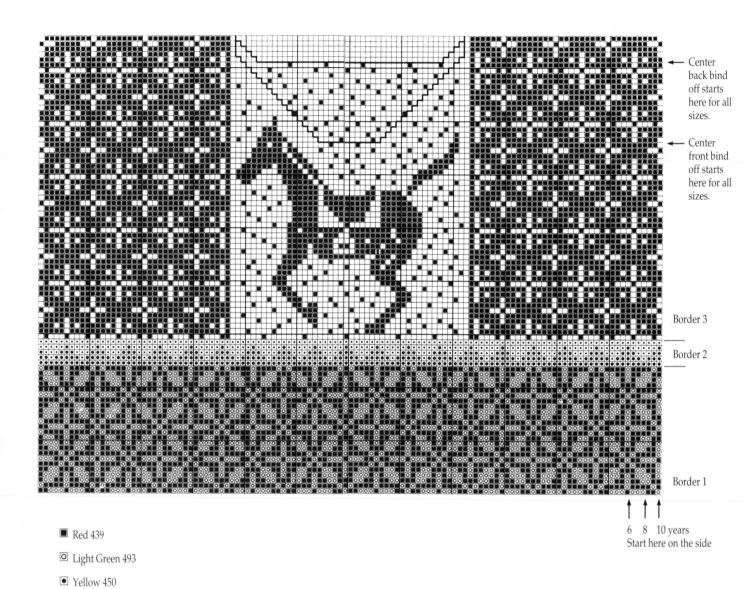

Center
back bind
off starts
here for all
sizes.

Center
front bind
off starts
here for all
sizes.

Border 3

Border 2

Border 1

6 8 10 years
Start here on the side

■ Red 439

◙ Light Green 493

◘ Yellow 450

▫ Turquoise 483

□ Dark Green 485

Rooster

Sizes: 6 (8) 10 (12) years

Finished Measurements:

Chest: 32¼" (34⅝") 37¾" (40⅞")

Length: 17¼" (18½") 20" (22⅜")

Head circumference: 17¼" (17¼") 20⅜" (20⅜")

Yarn: Rauma Gammel Serie and Finullgarn

Blue #438 (Gammel Serie); 250 (300) 350 (400)g

Natural #451(Gammel Serie); 250 (250) 300 (300)g

Red #435 (Finullgarn); 50 (50) 100 (100)g

Gauge: 27 sts and 32 rows over pattern = 4 × 4 inches. Make a swatch to assure proper gauge.

Needle suggestion: Double-point and circular needles sizes 2 and 3 (2.5mm and 3mm), or size to obtain gauge.

Body: Using Red and smaller needle, cast on 180 (200) 220 (240) sts. Join, being careful not to twist sts. Knit 1½" for facing, then a "picot edge" to fold as follows: *Yarn over, k2tog*; repeat between *s around. Knit 2 rnds. Work Border 1 according to the chart. Two sts, one on each side, are marking sts and worked in Blue. All incs are on each side of the marking sts. Change to larger needle and work Border 2, increasing 1 st on each side of the marking sts every 4th rnd to 220 (240) 260 (280) sts. When the body measures 9¾" (11") 12½" (15"), start Border 3. Bind off sts for the neck according to the chart, casting on 3 sts over the bound-off sts on the next rnd. Purl the new sts every rnd using two strands. They are for machine stitching and cutting later on. Keep working in the rnd. Continue shaping for the neck according to the chart by decreasing on each side of the 3 purl sts. After binding off sts for the back neck, work back and forth. The comb can be knit in Red, or duplicate stitched afterwards. Finish the chart and bind off or put remaining sts on holders.

Sleeves: Make 2. Using Red and smaller needles, cast on 43 (43) 45 (45) sts. Join, being careful not to twist sts. Work the facing and the "picot edge" as for the body. Change to larger needles. The first st on the rnd is the marking st, and is worked in Blue every rnd. Inc 1 st on each side of the marking st every other rnd until 57 (61) 63 (65) sts. Then dec every 3rd rnd until 119 (125) 135 (145) sts remain. Work until the sleeve measures 13¾" (15⅜") 16⅞" (20"). Finish at a suitable place on the chart. Purl 8 rnds for facing, increasing 2 sts at underarm every rnd. Bind off.

Finishing: For details on finishing, see Knitting Techniques on page 11. Machine stitch and cut for sleeve neck openings. Sew or graft the shoulders together. Using Blue, pick up sts around the neck and knit 1 rnd. Change to Red and knit 2 rnds, then 1 rnd "picot edge" as for the body. Knit 8 rnds, increasing 1 st at each corner of the front neck, and 2 sts at each corner of the back neck. Bind off. Sew in the sleeves. Weave all loose ends into the back of the fabric and sew the facings to the wrong side. Steam lightly. Duplicate stitch the comb if you did not knit it in.

Hat: 6/8 (10/12) years. Check your gauge. A small difference in gauge can make

a big difference in the finished size. Using Red and larger needle, cast on 120 (140) sts. Join, being careful not to twist sts. Work facing and picot edge as for the body. Work Border 1, then Border 2, omitting the center motif. Work until the hat measures 6¼" from the "picot edge". Bind off 1 st at center front, and 1 st at center back, and finish each side separately, working back and forth. Bind off 2 sts each time you turn. Work until no sts remain. Finish the other side. Graft the corners together, and sew the facing to the wrong side. Make a Red pompom and sew to each peak.

Stockings: 6/8 (10/12) years. Make 2. Using Red and smaller needles, cast on 60 (68) sts. Join, being careful not to twist sts. Work k1 through the back loop, p1 ribbing as follows: 2 rnds Red, then Blue until the ribbing measures 4" (4¾"). Change to larger needles, and inc evenly spaced to 68 (78) sts. The center back st is marking st, and is worked in Blue every rnd. Work Border 2, omitting the center motif. After 3⅛" (4"), start decreasing 1 st on each side of the

marking st every 6th (5th) rnd until 50 (54) sts remain. Work until the stocking measures 15¾" (18½"). Work the heel over sts on the first and the fourth needle, a total of 25 (27) sts. Work the heel in a stripe design, alternating 1 st each color. Work the heel 14 (16) rows long, finishing with a knit row.

Turning the heel: Purl until 2 sts beyond the center st, p2tog, p1. Turn. Knit until 2 sts beyond the center st, sl 1, k1, psso, k1. Turn. Purl until the st before the "hole", purl the st before and the st after the hole together, p1, turn. Knit until the st before the hole. Slip that st, knit the st after the hole, psso, k1, turn. Continue these two rows until all the sts on the outside of the hole are decreased—15 (17) sts remain. Pick up 10 (10) sts along each side of the heel and continue working in the rnd. Work the main design on the top of the foot, and the stripes under the foot decreasing as follows: Dec 1 st under the foot on each side every 4th rnd until 50 (54) sts remain. Work until the foot measures 6⅝" (7") or desired length, and work stripes all the way around. Dec 2 sts on each side of the foot until 8 sts remain. Put remaining sts on yarn, and fasten off.

Center front
Center back
Start here on the side for Border 3 6   8   10   12 years

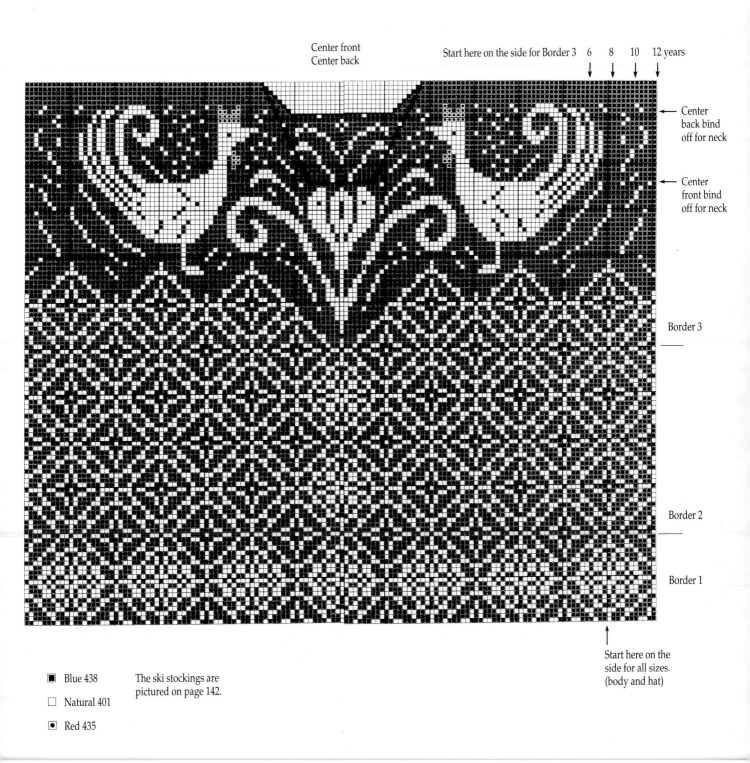

← Center
back bind
off for neck

← Center
front bind
off for neck

Border 3

Border 2

Border 1

↑
Start here on the
side for all sizes.
(body and hat)

■ Blue 438

□ Natural 401

▣ Red 435

The ski stockings are
pictured on page 142.

It is nice to stroll along the shore in the off season.
It rejuvenates the entire body to breathe fresh ocean air.
There are few people around when the water is too cold for swimming. You
can really do some thinking, peacefully staring at the horizon. With a
thermos filled with coffee for the adults,
and spade and a bucket for the little ones, you all can look
forward to some enjoyable hours. After a storm you can find
exciting things on the shore—seaweed, stones and sand,
pieces of wood rounded and shaped by the water, feathers,
and mysterious pieces of bones from animals or fish.
If you are really lucky, you may even find a message in a bottle!
Or maybe you'll send such a message yourself.
Warm knitted suits, hats, pants, or sweaters are just as nice
on a cool day at the shore as they are on a cold day in the mountains
or in the woods.

MODEL 16

Green Star Pullover

Sizes: 3 (6) 12 months

Finished Measurements:

Chest: 21¼" (22") 23⅝"

Length, pullover: 10¼" (11") 12½"

Waist, pants: 18⅛" (19⅝") 21¼"

Head circumference: 13¾" (14½") 15⅜"

Yarn: Rauma Babygarn

Pullover:

Green #B84; 100 (100) 150g

Rose #B56; 50 (50) 50g

Light Rose #B79; 50 (50) 50g

Purple #B42; 50 (50) 50g

Light Purple #B96; 50 (50) 50g

White #B11; 50 (50) 50g

Pants:

Green #B84; 100 (150) 200g

Hood, hat, mittens, socks:

Green #B84; 100 (100) 100g

plus small amounts of the other colors

Gauge: 32 sts and 38 rows over pattern = 4 × 4 inches. 31 sts and 40 rows over stockinette st = 4 × 4 inches. Make a swatch to assure proper gauge.

Needle suggestion: Double-point and circular needles sizes 0 and 2 (2mm and 2.5mm), or size to obtain gauge.

Body: Using Purple and smaller needle, cast on 172 (180) 192 sts. Join, being careful not to twist sts. Knit 7 rnds for facing, purl 1 rnd, then knit 1 rnd. Two sts, one on each side, are marking sts. They are worked in Green whenever possible. Change to larger needle and work Border 1 for 75 (83) 99 rnds, or until the body measures 7⅞" (8⅝") 10¼" from the purl rnd. Work Border 2. Bind off center front 33 (37) 39 sts for front neck according to the chart. On the next rnd, cast on 2 sts over the bound-off sts, and keep working in the rnd. Purl the new sts using two strands. They will be machine stitched and cut open later on. When the body measures approximately 9⅜" (10¼") 11¾", bind off center back 33 (37) 39 sts. Now you can either finish the body working back and forth or cast on 2 sts over the bound-off sts, and purl them using two strands as the front. Complete Border 2 finishing with 1 rnd Purple. Put the sts on holders or bind off.

Sleeves: Make 2. Using Purple and smaller needles, cast on 46 (46) 52 sts. Join, being careful not to twist sts. Knit 7 rnds for facing, purl 1 rnd, then knit 1 rnd. Change to larger needles and work Border 1 according to the chart, starting as indicated for your size. The first st on the rnd is a marking st, and is worked in Green whenever possible. Start underarm incs after the 3rd rnd. Inc 1 st on each side of the marking st every other rnd 11 (12) 4 times, then every 3rd rnd 13 (15) 23 times. Work until the sleeve measures 7" (7⅞") 8⅝". Using Green, knit 1 rnd, purl 1 rnd, then knit 7 rnds for facing. Bind off.

Finishing: For details on finishing, see Knitting Techniques on page 11. Steam the body and the sleeves carefully. Machine stitch and cut for sleeve openings. Sew or graft the shoulders together, making sure the Purple rnd shows. Machine stitch and cut for neck opening. Using Purple and smaller needles, pick up sts around the neck. Knit 6 rnds, decreasing 1 st at each corner every other rnd. Purl 1 rnd, then knit 8 rnds, increasing 1 st at each corner every other rnd. Bind off. Sew in the sleeves. Weave all loose ends into the back of the fabric and sew the facings to the wrong side.

Pants: Start at the waist and work down. Using Green and smaller needle, cast on 144 (156) 168 sts. Join, being careful not to twist sts. Work k1, p1 ribbing in the rnd for 3/4". Purl 1 rnd, then another 3/4" ribbing. Change to larger needle. Make the pants higher in the back to make them fit well. Place a marker at the beginning of the rnd. This marker is center back. Knit 8 sts. Turn. Slip the first st, purl until 8 sts beyond the marker. Turn. Slip the first st, knit until 16 sts beyond the marker. Turn. Work 8 sts more on each side until you have worked 40 sts beyond the marker on each side. Now Join, being careful not to twist sts. Mark the 2 center front and the 2 center back sts. Inc on each side of these marking sts. Inc 2 sts at center back every 3rd rnd 5 (6) 6 times. Then work even until the pants measure 6⅝" (7½") 8¼" from the purl rnd. Now inc 2 sts at center front and center back every other rnd 5 times.

Legs: Work the legs separately. Put half of the sts for one leg on a holder—from center front to center back. To shape the crotch, dec 1 st after the first and before the last st every other rnd 9 times, every 4th rnd 4 times, then every 5th rnd until 42 (46) 50 sts remain. Work until the leg measures 8¼" (9") 10¼". Change to smaller needles. Purl 1 rnd, then knit 7 rnds for facing.

Finishing: Steam carefully on the wrong side. Sew the leg facings to the wrong side. Sew the waistband to the wrong side, leaving a small opening for elastic. Weave all loose ends into the back of the fabric.

Hat: Check your gauge. A small difference in gauge can make a big difference in the finished size. Using Green and smaller needles, cast on 112 (118) 124 sts. Join, being careful not to twist sts. Knit 21 rnds for facing. Change to Purple, knit 2 rnds, purl 1 rnd, and knit 2 rnds. Change to larger needles and work the star border of Border 2 using Green and White. Work the first st on the rnd in Green every rnd. Using Purple, knit 1 rnd, increasing evenly spaced to 116 (124) 132 sts. Divide the hat into 4 sections with 29 (31) 33 sts in each section. The 2 first sts in each section are marking sts, and are worked in Green whenever possible. Work Border 1. Start according to the chart for your size. Inc 1 st on each side of the marking sts every other rnd 3 times, then every rnd 14 times. Using Green, knit 1 rnd, purl 1 rnd, and knit 1 rnd. Continue working Border 1, decreasing 1 st every rnd on each side of the marking sts. Do this until 21 sts rem in each section. Using Green, continue decreasing until 12 sts remain. Put remaining sts on yarn, and gather. Fasten off. Sew the facing to the wrong side.

Hood: Using Green and larger needle, cast on 242 sts. Join, being careful not to twist sts. Work k1, p1 ribbing for 4 rnds. Knit 1 rnd. *K9, k2tog*; repeat between *s around. Knit 4 rnds even. *K8, k2tog*; repeat between *s around. Knit 4 rnds even. Continue working 1 st less between each dec, and 4 rnds even between each dec rnd until 4 sts remain between decreases. You have a total of 112 sts. Change to smaller needles. Work k1, p1 ribbing for 2". Put 20 sts on a holder. Change to larger needles and work stockinette st back and forth. Bind off 2 sts on each side every other row 2 times, and 1 st on each side 2 times. Work until the hood measures 4¼" (4¾") 5⅛" from the purl rnd. To shape the hood, work as you do turning a

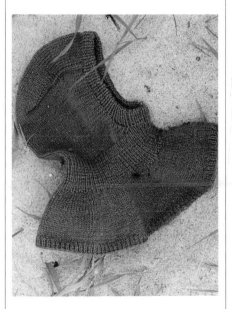

heel. Mark the 24 center sts on the needle. Start from the knit side. *Knit until the last st before the first marker. Knit the st before and the st after the marker together. Turn. Slip the first st. Purl until the last st before the marker on the other side. Purl the last st before the marker and the first st after the marker together. Turn*; repeat between *s until all the sts outside the "hole" on each side are decreased. Do not bind off. Pick up sts on each side in addition to the sts from the holder at center front. Change to smaller needles and work k1, p1 ribbing for 1½". Bind off loosely, and fold to the wrong side. Sew the facing, making a double ¾" brim around the the face opening. Weave all loose ends into the back of the fabric.

Socks: 3/6 (12) months. Make 2. Using Green and smaller needles, cast on 48 (48) sts. Join, being careful not to twist sts. Work k1, p1 ribbing for 4 rnds. Change to larger needles and work Border 2 according to the chart. The first st on each rnd is worked in Green. After Border 1, the sock is worked in Green only. Purl 1 rnd. Change to smaller needles and dec evenly spaced to 40 (44) sts. Knit 5 rnds. Turn the sock inside out, so the knit side of the cuff show when folded. Work k1, p1 ribbing until the sock measures 2¼" from the purl rnd. Change to larger needles and dec evenly spaced to 36 (40) sts. Knit for 4 rnds.

Heel: Place the sts from the first and the fourth needle on one needle, a total of 18 (20) sts. Work stockinette st back and forth over those sts for 18 (20) rows, slipping the first st of every row. Finish with a knit row.

Turning the heel: Mark the 2 center sts. Purl until 2 sts beyond the 2 center sts, p2tog, p1, turn. Slip the first st, knit until 2 sts beyond the center sts, sl 1, k1, psso, k1, turn. *Slip the first st, purl until the last st before the hole, purl that st and the st after the hole together, purl 1, turn. Slip the first st, knit until the last st before the hole. Slip that st, knit the st after the hole, pass the slip stitch over, knit 1, turn*; repeat between *s until all the sts on the outside of the hole are decreased. Pick up 10 (11) sts in the loops on

the sides of the heel and continue working in the rnd. The first and the fourth needle now have more sts than the second and the third needle. Dec 1 st at the end of the first needle and at the beginning of the fourth needle every other rnd until all the needles have the same number of sts. Work until the foot, including the heel, measures 3⅛" (3¾").

Shaping the toe: First needle: Knit the last 2 sts together. Second needle: Knit the first st, and pass the last st from needle 1 over. Knit across. Third needle: Knit the last 2 sts together. Fourth needle: Knit the first st, and pass the last st (the k2tog st) on needle 3 over. Knit across. Dec 4 sts like this every rnd until 8 sts remain. Put remaining sts on yarn, gather, and fasten off. Weave all loose ends into the back of the fabric.

Mittens: One size. Make 2. Using Purple and smaller needles, cast on 40 sts. Join, being careful not to twist sts. Knit 4 rnds for facing. Next rnd: *K2tog, yarn over*, repeat between *s around. Change to larger needles and work according to the chart. After the small star border, make another "yarn over" rnd: *K2tog, yarn over*; repeat between *s around. Continue working according to the chart. Dec on each side of a side st as shown on the chart. Put remaining sts on yarn, gather, and finish off. Sew the facing to the wrong side. Using Green, twist a cord and thread through the holes in the second "yarn over" rnd.

MODEL 16

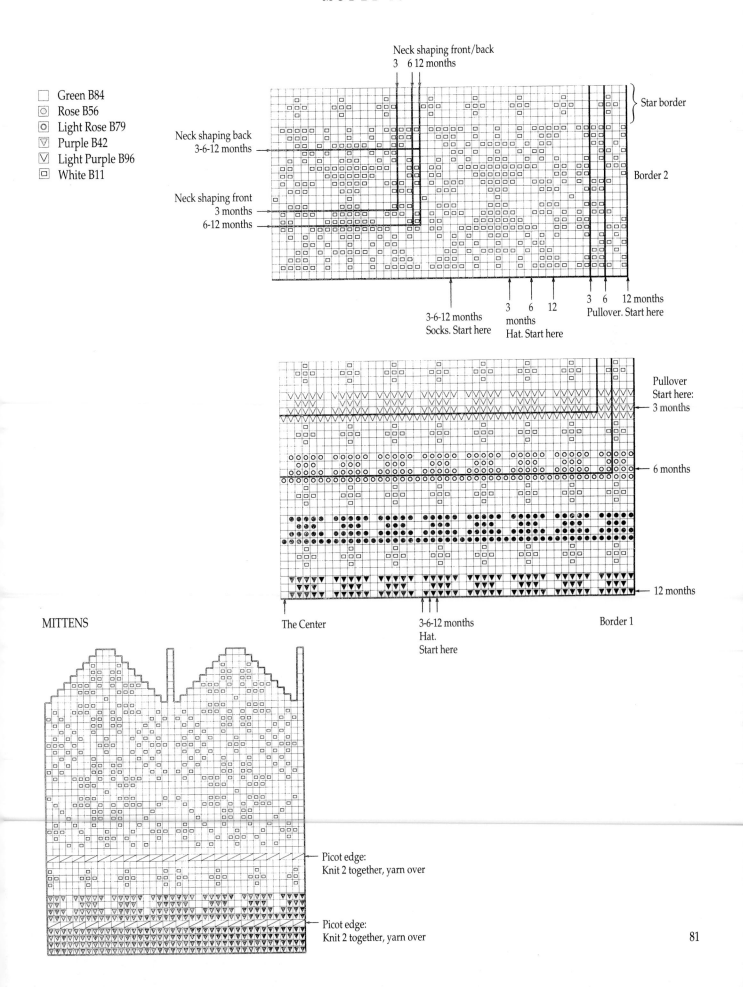

Green B84
Rose B56
Light Rose B79
Purple B42
Light Purple B96
White B11

Neck shaping front/back
3 6 12 months

Neck shaping back
3-6-12 months

Neck shaping front
3 months
6-12 months

Star border

Border 2

3-6-12 months
Socks. Start here

3
months
Hat. Start here

6   12

3 6   12 months
Pullover. Start here

Pullover
Start here:
3 months

6 months

12 months

The Center

3-6-12 months
Hat.
Start here

Border 1

MITTENS

Picot edge:
Knit 2 together, yarn over

Picot edge:
Knit 2 together, yarn over

81

MODEL 17

Yellow Cardigan with Borders

Sizes: 3 (6) 12 months

Finished Measurements:

Chest: 20⅜" (22") 25¼"

Length: 9¾" (10⅝") 13"

Yarn: Røros Lamullgarn

Yellow #L20; 100 (100, 100)g

Small amounts of:

Rose #L84

Dark Red #L47

Blue #L65

Light Blue #L51

Green #L83

This yarn goes a long way, so if you have any leftover in any of the colors, use that first.

Gauge: 29 sts and 33 rows over pattern = 4 × 4 inches. 32 sts and 45 rows over ribbing = 4 × 4 inches. Make a swatch to assure proper gauge.

Needle suggestion: Double-point and circular needles sizes 0 and 2 (2mm and 2.5mm), or size to obtain gauge.

Body: Using Yellow and smaller needle, cast on 145 (157) 181 sts. Work k1, p1 ribbing back and forth for 14 rows. Change to larger needle. Cast on 2 sts at the beginning of the row. Purl the new sts every rnd using two strands when two strands are in use in the rnd. The new sts will be machine stitched and cut open later on. Join, being careful not to twist sts and being working in the rnd. Count 33 (36) 42 sts after the center front purl sts. The next 2 sts are right side marking sts. Count the next 75 (81) 93 sts. The following 2 sts are the left side marking sts. The marking sts mark the sides between the fronts and the back, and are worked in Yellow whenever possible. Work Border 1. Start according to the chart for your size. After 64 (70) 88 rnds of Border 1, bind off the center front sts for front neck opening according to the chart. The 2 purl sts are not included on the chart, but they are bound off as well. Now you can either continue working in the rnd or back and forth. (See Knitting Techniques, "Neck openings", page 11.) After 70 (78) 96 rnds of Border 1, bind off center back sts for back neck according to the chart. Finish the Border according to the chart and bind off or put remaining sts on holders.

Sleeves: Make 2. Using Yellow and smaller double-point needles, cast on 42 (46) 50 sts. Join, being careful not to twist sts. Work k1, p1 ribbing for 14 rnds. Change to larger needles and inc evenly spaced to 57 (61) 67 sts. Work Border 2. The first 2 sts on the rnd are worked in Yellow every rnd, and the underarm incs are done on each side of these sts. Start underarm incs on the 4th rnd: Inc 2 sts every 3rd rnd 10 (3) 3 times, and every 4th rnd 0 (8) 11 times. Work until the sleeve measures 5⅛" (6") 8". Using Yellow, finish off by purling 1 rnd, then knitting 7 rnds for facing. Bind off.

Finishing: Weave all loose ends into the back of the fabric. If you worked in the rnd all the way up, you now have to cut the purl sts open. For details on finishing, see Knitting Techniques on page 11. Sew or graft the shoulders together. Sew in the sleeves, and sew the facing to the wrong side. Using Yellow and smaller needles, right side facing, pick up sts around the neck. Knit 1 row (or purl from the knit side). Work k1, p1 ribbing for 27 rows and bind off. Fold the neck band and sew to the wrong side to cover the cut edge.

Front bands: Using Yellow and smaller needle, right side facing, pick up sts along the left front edge. Knit 1 row from the purl side. Work k1, p1 ribbing for 13 rows. Bind off. Make buttonhole band to match, but after the 6th row, make 4 buttonholes evenly spaced. Make each buttonhole over 2 sts. Weave all loose ends into the back of the fabric and sew on 4 buttons.

Treatment of lamullgarn: Lamullgarn may seem loose and thin while working. But the yarn appears even and beautiful with proper aftercare.

Steaming can be a little rough. It is better to just soak the garment in mild soapy water. Use a detergent recommended for wool and lukewarm water. Rub the knit side of the garment carefully with suds, and rinse well. Lay the garment flat on a towel to dry.

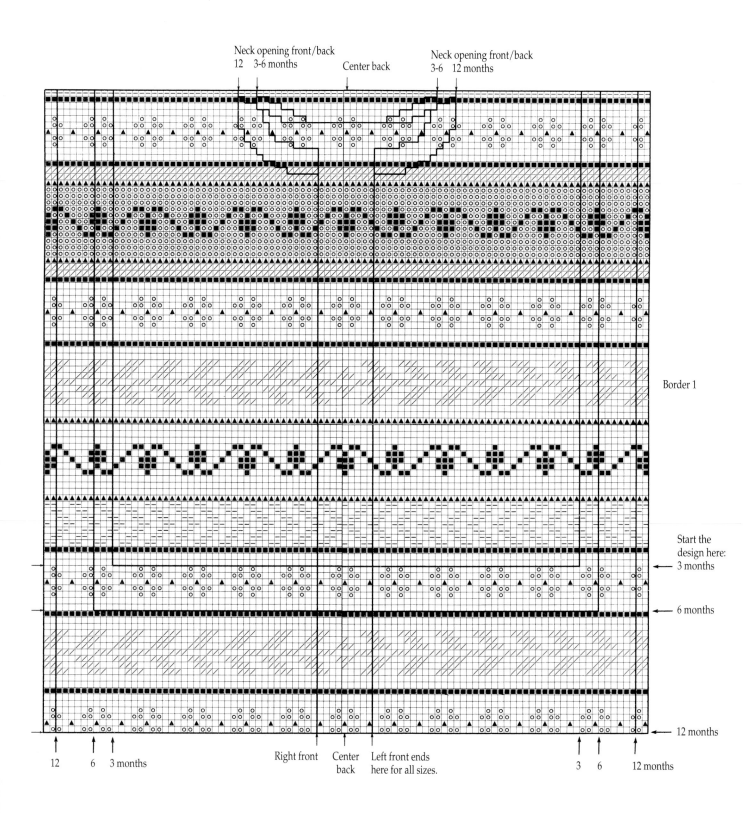

Neck opening front/back
12   3-6 months

Center back

Neck opening front/back
3-6   12 months

Border 1

Start the
design here:
3 months

6 months

12 months

12   6   3 months

Right front   Center   Left front ends
back   here for all sizes.

3   6   12 months

☐ Yellow L20
⊙ Light Blue L51
▲ Blue L65
⊘ Rose L84
■ Dark Red L47
⊟ Green L83

SLEEVE

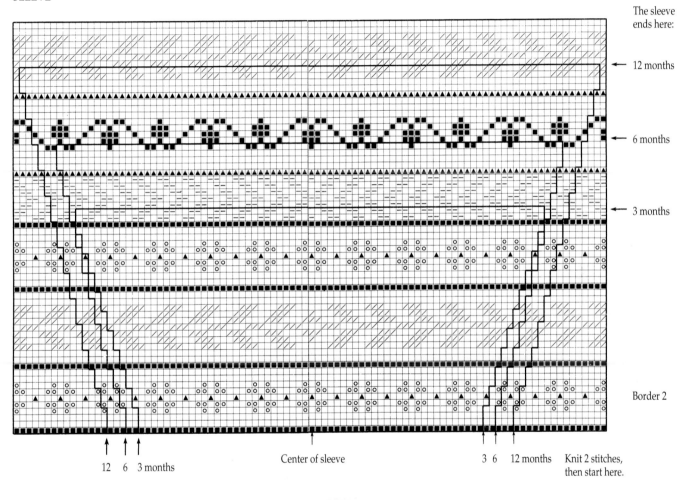

The sleeve
ends here:

← 12 months

← 6 months

← 3 months

Border 2

↑   ↑   ↑
12   6   3 months

Center of sleeve

3 6   12 months

Knit 2 stitches,
then start here.

Field of Flowers

Sizes: 1/2 (1) 2 years

Finished Measurements:

Chest: 24 3/8" (33") 38 1/2"

Length: 20 7/8" (23 5/8") 25 5/8"

Head circumference: 14 1/2" (16 1/8") 16 1/8"

Yarn: Rauma Babygarn

Violet #B42; 500 (550) 600g

Natural #B11; 300 (350) 400g

Gauge: 32 sts and 36 rows over pattern = 4 × 4 inches. Make a swatch to assure proper gauge.

Needle suggestion: Double-point and circular needles sizes 0 and 2 (2mm and 2.5mm), or size to obtain gauge.

Legs: Make 2. Using Violet and smaller needles, cast on 36 (48) 48 sts. Join, being careful not to twist sts. Work Border 1. Change to larger needles, increasing evenly spaced to 79 (89) 99 sts. Work Border 2, increasing 2 sts at the inseam every 3rd rnd to 123 (143) 163 sts. Work until the leg measures 9" (10¼") 11". Now dec for the crotch. Dec 2 sts to each side at the inseam every other rnd until 12 (14) 16 sts on each side are decreased.

Joining the legs: Put the sts for both the legs on one circular needle. The 2 center front sts are marking sts, and are purled every rnd using two strands. They are for machine stitching and cutting later on. The 2 center back sts are also marking sts. They are worked in Natural every rnd.

Body: Work until the suit measures 15⅜" (16⅞") 18⅞" from the crotch. Set aside and make the sleeves.

Sleeves: Make 2. Using Violet and smaller needles, cast on 24 (36) 36 sts. Join, being careful not to twist sts. Work Border 1. Change to larger needles, increasing evenly spaced to 49 (51) 57 sts. Work Border 2, and *at the same time* inc on each side of the center underarm st. Inc 2 sts at underarm every other rnd until 95 (109) 129 sts. Work until the sleeve measures 5½" (8⅝") 10⅝". Put the sts on holders.

Raglan shaping: Bind off 14 center underarm sts for each sleeve, and on each side of the body. Put all the pieces on one circular needle as follows: Front, sleeve, back, sleeve. The raglan decs take place 4 times each rnd, where the body and the sleeves meet. Two sts all 4 places (1 st from the body and 1 st from the sleeve) are worked in Natural every rnd, and the decs are done on each side of

these sts. Dec 1 st every rnd on the sleeve, and 1 st every other rnd on the body. Keep continuity of the design, and dec until 3 sts remain on the sleeves. Using Natural, knit 1 rnd, and put the sts on holders.

Finishing: For details on finishing, see Knitting Techniques on page 11. Machine stitch and cut for front opening. Sew the crotch seam and embroider 2 rows of chain sts on top of the seam. Chain st: Insert the needle from the wrong side, go through to the knit side. Bring the needle back to the wrong side through that same hole, leaving a loop on the knit side. Repeat the procedure 1

st apart, making sure the needle goes through the loop on the right side for every st. Using Natural, pick up the sts along the front openings and around the neck. Knit 1 rnd, then lace border: *Yarn over, k2tog, k2*; repeat between *s around. On the next rnd, k6 sts into each hole; alternate k1, p1 into each yarn over of the previous rnd. Knit 1 rnd, purl 1 rnd, bind off. Sew underarm. Make the lace border around the cuffs and also around the ankles. Sew on buttons at center front—the loops in the lace border serve as buttonholes. Weave all loose ends into the back of the fabric, and steam lightly.

Hat: 6 months (1 year/2 years). Check your gauge. A small difference in gauge can make a big difference in the finished size. Using Violet and smaller needles, cast on 120 (132) sts. Join, being careful not to twist sts. Work Border 1. Change to larger needles. Now inc, and *at the same time* work the "lice" (dots). There are 3 sts between each "lice" and 1 rnd of Violet between each "lice" rnd. Place a marker at st number 20 (22), 40 (44), 60 (66), 80 (88), 100 (110), and 120 (132); 6 markers placed as center markers. Inc 2 sts (1 st on each side of each marker) every rnd 20 times. Purl 1 rnd. Now dec 2 sts at each marker until 6 sts remain. Put remaining sts on yarn, gather, and finish off. Make the lace border around the hat.

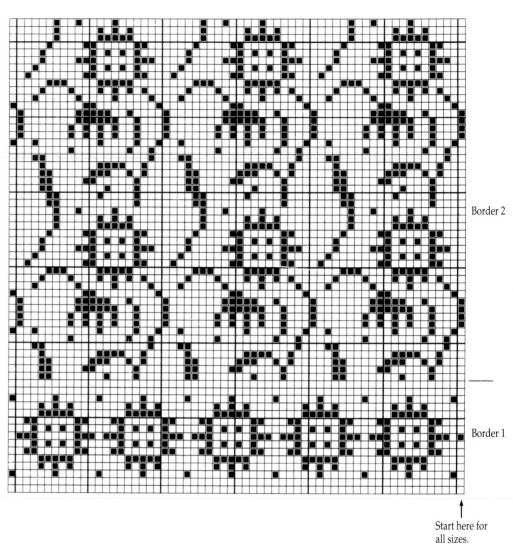

Border 2

Border 1

Start here for all sizes.

■ Natural B11

□ Violet B442

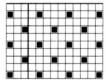

"Lus" (dots) design, hat

Heart Pullover and Tights

Sizes: 4 (6) 8 (10) years

Finished Measurements:

Chest: 29⅛" (31½") 34⅝" (38½")

Length: 18⅞" (20⅜") 22" (23⅝")

Hips, tights: 22" (23⅝") 24⅜" (26")

Length, tights: 24⅜" (27½") 31½" (32⅝")

Head circumference: 19¼" (19¼") 20⅛"
(20⅞")

Yarn: Rauma Finullgarn

Pullover:

Blue #437; 250 (300) 350 (400)g

Rose #4686; 50 (50) 50 (100)g

Red #439; 50 (50) 50 (100)g

Turquoise #483; 50 (50) 50 (100)g

Green #430; 50 (50) 50 (100)g

Yellow #450; 50 (50) 50 (50)g

Tights:

Turquoise #483; 250 (250) 300 (350)g

Yellow #450; 50 (50) 100 (100)g

Rose #4686; 50 (50) 100 (100)g

Red #439; 50 (50) 100 (100)g

Blue #437; 50 (50) 100 (100)g

Gauge: 27 sts and 32 rows over pattern = 4 ×
4 inches. Make a swatch to assure proper
gauge.

Needle suggestion: Double-point and circular needles sizes 2 and 3 (2.5mm and
3mm), or size to obtain gauge.

Body: Using Blue and larger needle, cast on 204 (216) 240 (264) sts. Join, being careful not to twist sts. Work Border 1 according to the chart; first Yellow hearts, then alternately Rose/Red and Green/Turquoise hearts. Work until the pullover measures 16⅛" (17¾") 19¼" (20⅞"). Bind off center front 40 (40) 42 (44) sts for front neck. Work back and forth, and *at the same time* dec 1 st on each side of the neck. (For details on neck openings, see Knitting Techniques on page 00). Dec a total of 4 sts on each side. Then bind off center back 48 (48) 50 (52) sts for back neck. Finish each side separately and work back and forth for 1". Bind off.

Sleeves: Make 2. Using Blue and larger needles, cast on 39 (43) 45 (47) sts. Join, being careful not to twist sts. Work design as for the body. *At the same time* inc 2 sts at underarm every other rnd until 113 (119) 125 (135) sts. Work until the sleeve measures approximately 11" (13") 13¾" (15"). Finish with a heart border. Purl 6 rnds for facing, increasing 2 sts at underarm every rnd. Bind off.

Finishing: For details on finishing, see Knitting Techniques on page 11. Machine stitch and cut for sleeve openings. Sew the shoulders. Using Yellow and larger needle, pick up the sts around the neck for lace border. Knit 1 rnd. *Yarn over, k2tog, knit 2*; repeat between *s around. On the next rnd, work 6 sts into each hole (alternate k1, p1 into each yarn over of the previous rnd). Knit 1 rnd, purl 1 rnd, bind off. Make the same lace border around the bottom of the sweater, and around the cuffs. Sew in the sleeves. Weave all loose ends into the back of the fabric, and sew the facings to the wrong side. Steam lightly.

Hat: 4–6 (8–10) years. Check your gauge. A small difference in gauge can make a big difference in the finished size. Using Yellow and larger needle, cast on 132 (144) sts. Join, being careful not to twist sts. Knit in the rnd for 1½", then picot edge: *Yarn over, k2tog*; repeat between *s around. Knit 2 rnds. Change to Blue and work the Yellow hearts

from Border 1. Change to Turquoise and inc evenly spaced to 180 (198) sts. Work Border 2 for 6⅝". Put remaining sts on yarn, gather, and fasten off. Make a Red pompom, and sew to the top of the hat. Weave all loose ends into the back of the fabric and sew the facing to the wrong side. Steam lightly.

Tights: Using Turquoise and smaller needle, cast on 150 (162) 168 (180) sts. Join, being careful not to twist sts. Knit casing for elastic for 1⅛", purl 1 rnd, then knit for another 1⅛". Change to larger needle and work Border 2 according to the chart. When the tights measure 8⅝" (9⅜") 10¼" (11") from the purl rnd, inc 2 sts at center front and center back every other rnd until 170 (182) 186 (198) sts. Put 85 (91) 93 (99) sts— from center front to center back—on holders. Work in the rnd on remaining sts to finish one leg. At the inseam, dec 2 sts every 4th rnd 14 (14) 12 (12) times, then 2 sts every 9th (12th) 12th (12th) rnd 6 (6) 9 (9) times. Work until the leg measures 13¾" (16⅛") 19¼" (19⅝"), or desired length. Using Turquoise, work k1 through the back loop, p1 ribbing for 1⅛", and finish with a lace border as for the pullover. Sew the facing to the wrong side, put in elastic, weave all loose ends into the back of the fabric, and steam lightly.

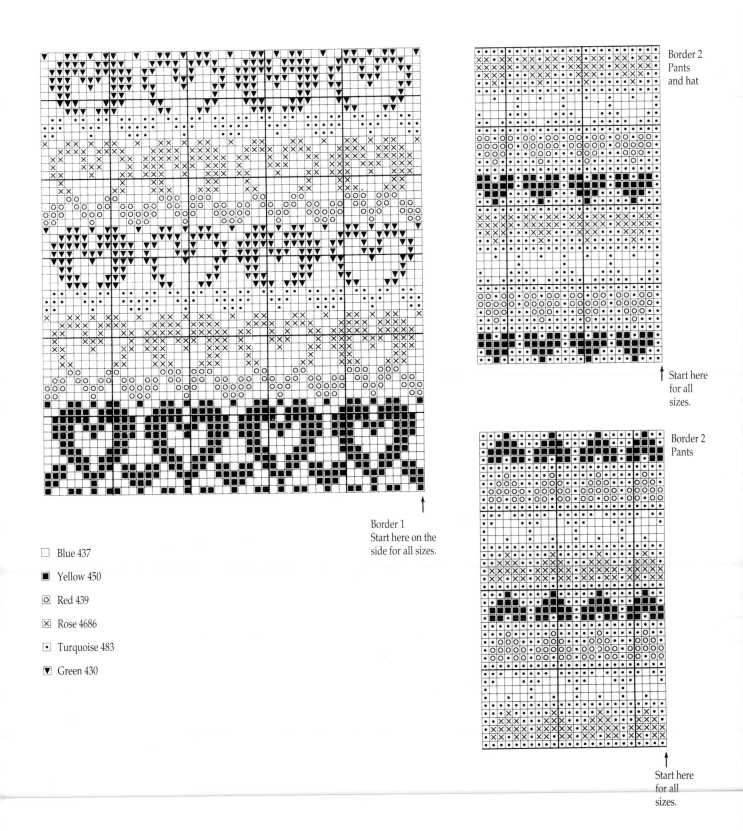

Border 2
Pants
and hat

↑ Start here
for all
sizes.

Border 2
Pants

Border 1
Start here on the
side for all sizes.

☐ Blue 437

■ Yellow 450

◉ Red 439

☒ Rose 4686

⊡ Turquoise 483

▼ Green 430

↑ Start here
for all
sizes.

On festive days when we are out and about,
it is great to have warm festive clothes.
Have you been cold in the rain on Independence Day?
Have you thought we will not have a summer this year,
because a cold wind made us stay inside the first day of summer?
With these tough warm festive clothes, children are dressed for
any occasion, from chilly spring afternoons to the cold evenings
of December when the Christmas tree is lit.
The little hooded suit is just as nice on a festive occasion
as for a casual stroll.

MODEL 20

Joyous Colors

Sizes: 1 (2) 3 (4) years

Finished Measurements:

Chest: 23⅝" (26¾") 28¼" (29⅞")

Length, cardigan: 12½" (14⅛") 15" (16½")

Hips, pants: 22¾" (23⅝") 24⅜" (25¼")

Length, pants: 17¼" (18½") 20⅜" (22⅜")

Yarn: Rauma Finullgarn

Green #430; 150 (150) 200 (300)g

Yellow #450; 100 (100) 150 (150)g

Red #439; 100 (100) 150 (150)g

Orange #460; 100 (100) 150 (150)g

Rose #4886; 100 (100) 150 (150)g

Charcoal #4387; 50 (100) 100 (100)g

Gauge: 27 sts and 32 rows over pattern = 4 × 4 inches. Make a swatch to assure proper gauge.

Needle suggestion: Double-point and circular needles sizes 2 and 3 (2.5mm and 3mm), or size to obtain gauge.

Body: Using Charcoal and smaller needle, cast on 146 (158) 170 (197) sts. Join, being careful not to twist sts. The 2 center front sts are purled every rnd using two strands. They are for machine stitching and cutting later on. Knit 1½" in the rnd for facing, purl 1 rnd, and knit 2 rnds. Work Border 1. Change to larger needle and inc evenly spaced to 158 (182) 194 (206) sts.

Work Border 2 until the cardigan measures 8⅝" (8⅝") 9⅜" (11"). Start Border 3. Put 18 (19) 19 (19) sts from each side of the purl sts on holders for neck/hood as follows: Size 1 year: In the middle of the 1st repeat of Border 3; Sizes 2, 3, 4 years: after the 1st repeat of Border 3. Continue working in the rnd. Continue purling the center front sts every rnd using two strands. In the middle of the 2nd, (3rd) 3rd (3rd) repeat, bind off center back 36 (38) 38 (38) sts for back neck. Work back and forth until the end of the repeat. (For details on neck openings, see Knitting Techniques on page 11). Bind off.

Sleeves: Make 2. Using Charcoal and smaller needles, cast on 39 (42) 45 (45) sts. Join, being careful not to twist sts. Work the facing and Border 1 as the body. Change to larger needles, and inc evenly spaced to 43 (47) 51 (55) sts. Work Border 2, and *at the same time* inc 2 sts at underarm every other rnd to 85 (97) 109 (113) sts. Work until the sleeve measures 9" (9¾") 10⅝" (11⅜"). Purl 8 rnds for facing, increasing 2 sts underarm every rnd. Bind off.

Finishing: For details on finishing, see Knitting Techniques on page 11. Machine stitch and cut open at center front. Using Green, pick up sts along one front and work the front band as the 6 first rows of Border 1. Put the sts on holders. Make the other front band the same. Machine st and cut for sleeve openings. Sew the shoulders. Pick up the front neck sts from the holders and pick up the sts from the front bands. Finish each side separately, working back and forth. Work Border 1, increasing 1 st to the neck side every other row until you reach the shoulder seam. Put aside while finishing the other front band. Now pick up sts around the back neck, and put all the sts on one needle: left front of the hood, back neck, and right front of the hood. Bind off 10 sts on each side of the opening. On the next rnd, cast on 3 sts over the bound-off sts. Purl these sts using

two strands so you can join, being careful not to twist sts. The 3 sts are for machine stitching and cutting later on. Work for 7⅞". Bind off the 3 cutting sts, and on the next rnd cast on 20 sts over the bound-off sts. Keep working in the rnd, and at the same time bind off 2 sts on each side every 3rd rnd. Work and bind off until 8 sts remain. Put remaining sts on yarn, gather, and fasten off. Machine stitch and cut open along the purl sts. Using Charcoal, work a continuous facing all the way around the front opening: Pick up the sts from the left front band holder. Pick up sts around the hood opening and from the right front band holder. Knit 1 rnd, purl 1 rnd, then knit, decreasing 2 sts at each front band corner, and increasing 2 sts at each hood opening corner. Knit 8 rnds. Bind off. Weave all loose ends into the back of the fabric, sew the facing to the wrong side, and steam lightly. Make a Charcoal pompom and sew to the top of the hood. Sew hooks and eyes on the inside of the front bands.

Pants: Using Charcoal and smaller needles, cast on 45 (48) 48 (51) sts. Work facing and Border 1 as the body. Change to larger needles, increasing evenly spaced to 69 (79) 89 (99) sts. Now inc 2 sts at the inseam every 3rd rnd. Work Border 2, increasing until 97 (109) 119 (129) sts. Work until the leg measures 10¼" (11") 12½" (14⅛"). Now bind off for the crotch. Bind off 12 sts, 6 each side of the inseam. Then bind off 2 sts each side every other row 3 (4) 5 (6) times. You have now bound off 12 (14) 16 (18) sts on each side. Make another leg the same. Put the sts from both legs on one circular needle. Dec sts so the design comes out right at center front and center back. Work until the pants

measure 15¾" (16⅞") 18⅞" (20⅞"). Change to smaller needle and work Border 1. Using Charcoal, knit 1 rnd, purl 1 rnd, and knit 14 rnds for casing for the elastic. Bind off. Sew the crotch seam. Weave all loose ends into the back of the fabric, sew the casing to the wrong side, put in elastic, and steam lightly.

☐ Green 430

◉ Yellow 450

☒ Red 439

■ Orange 460

● Rose 4886

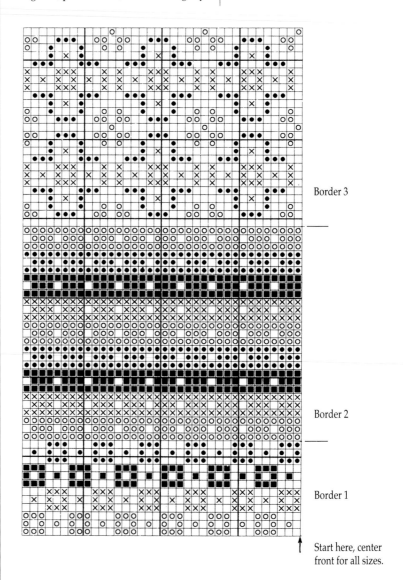

Border 3

Border 2

Border 1

Start here, center front for all sizes.

MODEL 21

Festive Dress and Cardigan

Sizes: 2 (4) 6 (8) years

Finished Measurements:

Chest, dress: 21¼" (24⅜") 26" (27½")

Length, dress: 22" (27¼") 32¼" (36⅝")

Chest, cardigan: 19⅝" (23⅝") 26" (27½")

Length, cardigan: 9" (10⅝") 11¾" (13")

Yarn: Rauma Finullgarn

Dress:

Black #436; 200 (250) 300 (350)g

Red #435; 100 (150) 200 (250)g

Green #421; 50 (50) 50 (50)g

Orange #469; 50 (50) 50 (50)g

Blue #467; 50 (50) 50 (50)g

Yellow #450; 100 (100) 150 (200)g

Cardigan:

Red #435; 250 (300) 350 (400)g

Black #436; 50 (50) 100 (100)g

Green #421; 50 (50) 50 (50)g

Yellow #450; 50 (50) 50 (50)g

Gauge: 27 sts and 32 rows over pattern = 4 × 4 inches. Make a swatch to assure proper gauge.

Needle suggestion: Double-point and circular needles size 3 (3mm), or size to obtain gauge.

Dress: Using Blue, cast on 220 (260) 300 (320) sts. Join, being careful not to twist sts. Knit 1⅛" for facing, purl 1 rnd, then work Border 1. Continue working Border 2 until the garment measures 15" (18⅞") 22¾" (26"). Dec evenly spaced to 145 (167) 178 (189) sts. Make the 2 center front marking sts. They are for machine stitching and cutting later on. They are purled every rnd using two strands. Using Blue, knit 2 rnds, then Border 3 for 4" (4¼") 4¾" (5⅛"). Bind off 10 sts on each side, and cast on 2 sts over the bound-off sts on the next rnd. Purl these 2 sts every rnd using two strands. When the bodice measures 4" (5⅛") 6¼" (7½"), start shaping for V-neck. Work in the rnd, decreasing 1 st on each side of the center front purl sts every other rnd. Work and dec until the garment measures 7" (8¼") 9⅜" (10⅝"). Now bind off as many sts at center back for back neck as you have decreased altogether for the front neck. Work back and forth for 3/4", decreasing 1 st every other row each side of the front neck and the back neck. For details on neck openings, see Knitting Techniques on page 00. Bind off.

Finishing: For details on finishing, see Knitting Techniques on page 11. Machine stitch and cut for front and sleeve openings. Sew the shoulders together. Using Blue, pick up sts along one front, around the neck, and along the other front. Work the facing back and forth. Knit 1 row from the knit side, knit 1 row from the purl side, work 6 rows stockinette stitch, increasing 2 sts at the back neck curves, and decreasing 1 st at the front neck corners. Bind off. Using Blue, pick up the sts around the sleeve openings. Knit 1 rnd, purl 1 rnd, then knit 6 rnds for facing, increasing 2 sts at each corner every rnd. Bind off. Weave all loose ends into the back of the fabric. Sew the facing to the wrong side, and steam lightly.

Cardigan: The cardigan is worked from cuff to cuff. It is worked in the rnd, except for the center back, which is as wide as the front opening. You will cut the the bottom open later. Using Green, cast on 27 (35) 39 (43) sts. Join, being careful not to twist sts. Knit 1½" for facing. Purl 1 rnd and knit 2 rnds. Work Border 4 for 1½", then start the underarm incs. Inc 1 st on each side of the underarm center st every 3rd rnd until 37 (47) 49 (53) sts are on the needles. Then inc every rnd to 125 (145) 163 (179) sts. Work until the garment measures 8¼" (9½") 11⅜" (13⅜"). You have now finished the sleeve, and are starting the body. Keep working in the rnd, but cast on 3 sts over the center st. These sts are purled every rnd. They are for machine stitching and cutting later on. Work in the rnd until the garment measures 11¾" (14⅛") 16½" (18⅞"). Start Border 5. Shape for front neck as shown on the chart. Bind off 68 (78) 88 (92) sts, including the 3 purl sts. Work the repeat back and forth according to the chart. Now cast on 68 (78) 88 (92) sts, including 3 purl sts at the bottom, and join, being careful not to twist sts. As shown on the chart, Border 5 is now mirror imaged. Work to the same place as you casted on the purl sts on the opposite side. Now bind off the 3 purl sts and work the other sleeve. Dec as you increased on the other sleeve: Dec 2 sts every rnd until 37 (47) 49 (53) sts remain. Then dec 2 sts every 3rd rnd until 27 (35) 39 (43) sts remain. Work 1½". Work the border and facing as the first sleeve. Bind off. Machine stitch along the purl sts and cut the bottom open. If it is difficult to sew through the cuff opening, cut a hole big enough to fit the sewing machine foot into at the bottom, near the marking st first, so it is easier to do the machine stitching. Using Green, pick up sts all the way around the opening (cardigan) in one piece. Knit 2 rnds, purl 1 rnd, then knit 8 rnds, decreasing 2 sts at the lower corners of the opening, and increasing 2 sts at the bottom of the sides and at the back neck corners. Bind off. Weave all loose ends into the back of the fabric, sew the facings to the wrong side, and steam lightly.

☐ Black 436

■ Red 435

■ Orange 469

☒ Blue 467

⊡ Yellow 450

⊡ Green 421

DRESS

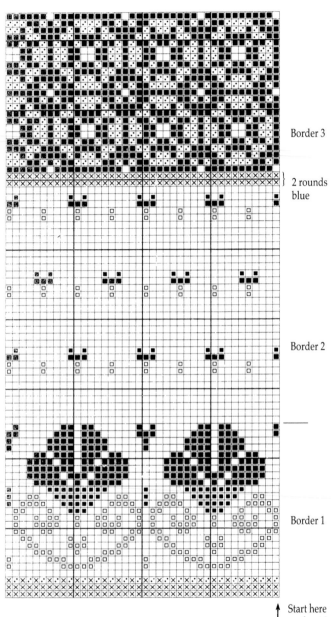

Border 3

} 2 rounds blue

Border 2

Border 1

↑ Start here on the side for all sizes

CARDIGAN

Bind off for front
neck opening
Work this piece
back and forth

Border 5

Border 4

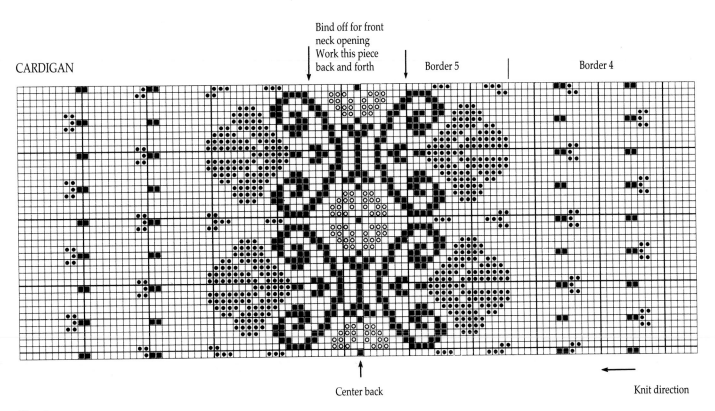

Center back

Knit direction

☐ Red 435

⦿ Black 436

■ Green 421

◎ Yellow 450

Festive Cardigan and Knickers

Sizes: 2 (4) 6 (8) years

Finished Measurements:

Chest: 26¾" (30⅝") 33" (34⅝")

Length, cardigan: 11¾" (13¾") 14½" (15¾")

Hips, knickers: 21¼" (25¼") 26¾" (28¼")

Length, knickers: 13¾" (17¼") 20⅞" (24⅜")

Head circumference: 16⅛" (18⅛") 18⅛" (20⅜")

Yarn: Rauma Finullgarn

Cardigan:

Red #435; 200 (250) 300 (350)g

Yellow #450; 200 (250) 300 (350)g

Blue #467; 50 (50) 50 (50)g

Black #436; 50 (50) 50 (100)g

Knickers:

Red #435; 50 (100) 100 (150)g

Yellow #450; 50 (100) 100 (150)g

Blue #467; 50 (50) 50 (50)g

Black #436; 150 (200) 250 (300)g

Gauge: 27 sts and 32 rows over pattern = 4 × 4 inches. Make a swatch to assure proper gauge.

Needle suggestion: Double-point and circular needles sizes 2 and 3 (2.5mm and 3mm), or size to obtain gauge.

Cardigan: Using Blue and smaller needle, cast on 128 (156) 170 (198) sts. Join, being careful not to twist sts. The 2 center front sts are marking sts and are purled every rnd. They are for machine stitching and cutting later on. Knit 1½" in the rnd for facing, purl 1 rnd, and knit 1 rnd. Work Border 1. Change to larger needle, and start Border 2. Each front takes 24 (31) 36 (42) sts, and the back takes 78 (92) 96 (112) sts. Make 1 st on each side a marking st. Knit these marking sts in Red, and inc on each side of them. The cardigan has complete repeats bordering the front openings as shown on the chart. Knit the design, and inc 1 st on each side of the marking sts every 4th rnd until 154 (182) 196 (210) sts. Work until the cardigan measures full length. Finish with a half or a complete repeat. Put the sts on holders.

Sleeves: Make 2. Using Blue and smaller needles, cast on 39 (41) 43 (45) sts. Join, being careful not to twist sts. Work facing and Border 1 as the body. Change to larger needles. Work Border 2, and *at the same time* inc 2 sts underarm every other rnd until 97 (113) 119 (125) sts are on the needles. Work until the sleeve measures 10⅝" (11⅜") 13" (13¾"). Finish with a half or a complete repeat. Purl 8 rnds for facing, increasing 2 sts underarm every rnd. Bind off.

Finishing: For details on finishing, see Knitting Techniques on page 11. Machine stitch and cut for front opening. Sew the bottom facing to the wrong side. Make the front bands. Using Black, pick up sts along the left front, starting at the lower corner, ending 1 repeat from the top. The number of sts must be divisible by 14. Cast on 3 sts, and purl them every rnd. Starting 1 repeat from the top, pick up the same number of sts down the right front. Cast on another 3 sts to

purl every rnd. Now you can knit the front bands in the rnd, machine stitching and cutting the purl sts later on. Work 1 repeat of Border 1. Then, using Blue, knit 1 rnd, purl 1 rnd, and knit 18 rnds for facing. Bind off. Machine stitch and cut the purl sts. Put Border 1 and the 18 Blue facing rows right sides together. Sew the upper and the lower corners and turn inside out. Then sew the remaining Blue facing to the wrong side. Machine st and cut for sleeve openings. Graft the shoulders. Using Blue and larger needle, pick up sts around the neck opening. Knit 1 row from the knit side, knit 1 row from the purl side, then work 8 rows stockinette stitch for facing, increasing 2 sts every row at the corners of the back neck. Bind off, and sew the facing to the wrong side. Sew in the sleeves. Weave all loose ends into the back of the fabric, and steam lightly. Sew pewter clasps on the front.

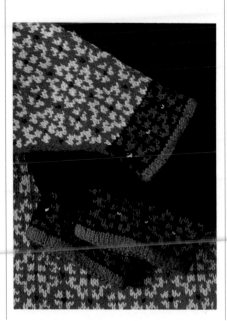

Knickers: Using Blue and smaller needles, cast on 51 (55) 60 (65) sts. Join, being careful not to twist sts. Knit 11 rnds for facing. Purl 1 rnd and knit 1 rnd. Work Border 1. Change to Black and larger needles, and inc evenly spaced to 71 (75) 81 (85) sts. Make the center st at the inseam a marking st. Inc 1 st on each side of this st every 3rd rnd until 97 (109) 113 (121) sts. Work until the leg measures 5⅞" (8¼") 10⅝" (13").

Shaping the crotch: From the center st, bind off 9 (9) 9 (11) sts on the back, and 5 (5) 5 (6) sts on the front. Work back and forth, decreasing 1 st on each side every time you turn, 4 times—75 (87) 91 (96) sts remain. Make another leg the same, but make sure the crotch decreases are mirror-imaged. Put all the sts on one needle and work in the rnd for 4¾" (5⅞") 7" (8¼"). Now dec evenly spaced to 140 (162) 172 (189) sts. Change to smaller needle. Using Blue, knit 2 rnds and 1 repeat of Border 1. Using Blue, knit 1 rnd, purl 1 rnd, and knit 11 rnds for casing for elastic. Bind off.

Vest: In the 2nd to last rnd of the casing (the 10th rnd) of the knickers waistline, using Blue and larger needle, pick up 57 (61) 61 (76) sts across the front, cast on 3 side marking sts, pick up same number of sts across the back, then cast on 3 additional side marking sts. Join, being careful not to twist sts. Purl the new sts every rnd using two strands. They are for machine stitching and cutting later on. Work Border 1, making sure the design is centered. Start Border 1 for 4" (5⅛") 6¼" (7½"), then start shaping for V-neck. Bind off 1 st at center front, and on the next rnd, cast on 2 sts over the bound-off st.

Purl the 2 sts every rnd using two strands. Dec 1 st on each side of the purl sts every other rnd until the vest measures 7" (8¼") 9⅜" (10⅝"). Then, at center back, bind off as many sts as you have decreased for the V-neck. Work back and forth for 3/4", decreasing 1 st on each side of the back neck and front neck every other row. For details on working designs back and forth, see Knitting Techniques, "Neck openings", on page 11.

Finishing: For details on finishing, see Knitting Techniques on page 11. Machine stitch and cut along the purl sts on the sides and for the neck. Using Blue and larger needles, pick up sts around the vest: Up along the left side, across the left shoulder, along both sides of the V-neck, across the right shoulder, and down the right side. Work back and forth. From the knit side, knit 1 row, and from the purl side, knit 1 row. Work 6 rows stockinette stitch, decreasing 2 sts every row at each corner between the sides and the shoulders, decreasing 1 st every row at the corners between the V-neck and the shoulders, and increasing every row 3 sts at the bottom of the V-neck. Bind off. Work the same facing on the back, decreasing 2 sts every row at the corners between the sides and the shoulders, and increasing every row 2 sts at each curve of the neck. Sew the facings to the wrong side. Sew the casing to the wrong side and put in elastic. Sew the crotch seam. Weave all loose ends into the back of the fabric. Using Blue and stem sts, embroider a continuation of the Blue stripe on the vest on each side, approximately 2" down, to give the impression of a flap. Steam lightly. Sew on decorative buttons, and clasps on the shoulders.

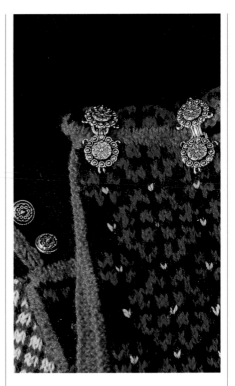

Hat: 2 (4/6) 8 years. Check your gauge. A small difference in gauge can make a big difference in the finished size. Using Blue and smaller needles, cast on 112 (126) 140 sts. Join, being careful not to twist sts. Work facing and border as the body. Change to larger needles. Work Border 3, but inc evenly spaced 2 (0) 1 st to make the design come out even. Work until the hat measures 6¼" from the purl rnd. Dec 1 st at center front and 1 st at center back. Put half of the sts (from dec to dec) on a holder. Work back and forth over remaining sts. Bind off 2 sts every time you turn until all the sts are bound off. Make the other half the same. Sew the two halves together, knit sides facing each other. Weave all loose ends into the back of the fabric and sew the facing to the wrong side. Steam lightly.

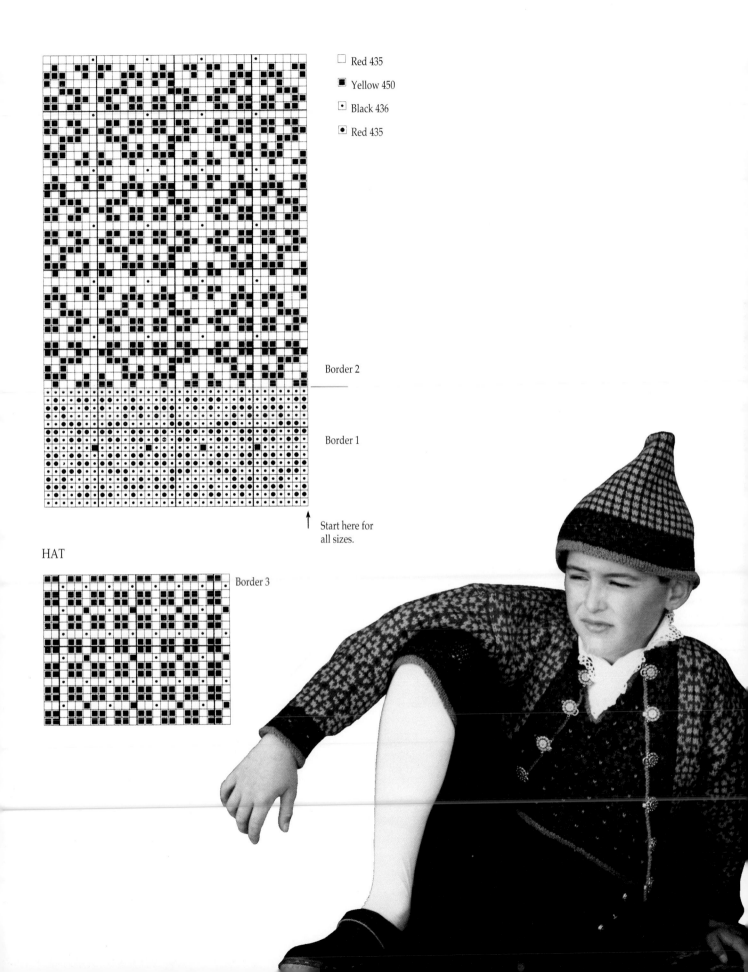

Red 435

Yellow 450

Black 436

Red 435

Border 2

Border 1

Start here for
all sizes.

HAT

Border 3

Young children admire older siblings.
Sighing and groaning, the older ones teach bothersome
brothers and sisters lots of things–like fishing, playing pirates on the pier,
catching crabs, and watching for jellyfish.
They look after the younger ones so they don't fall into the water,
and make sure they use a life jacket. They save them
from dangerous fights, and comfort them in hard times.
It does the older children good to care for the younger.
Siblings can have a good time together, even if the age difference is great.
A big hand-made pullover or cardigan is a great outfit for
crab fishermen, soccer players, race car drivers, roller skaters,
and adventurers of all types.

Small Fishing Pullover

Sizes: 1 (2) 3 years

Finished Measurements:

Chest: 23⅝" (26¾") 28¼"

Length: 13" (14⅛") 15"

Head circumference: 18⅛" (18⅞") 19⅝"

Yarn: Rauma Finullgarn

Colorway 1—Beige pullover

Color 1: Beige #406; 100 (150) 150g

Color 2: Blue #4385; 100 (100) 100g

Color 3: Grey Green #483; 100 (100) 100g

Color 4: Rose #4571; 50 (50) 50g

Color 5: Light Green #4887; 50 (50) 50g

Color 6: Dark Blue #482; 50 (50) 50g

Colorway 2—Blue pullover

Color 1: Dark Blue #482; 100 (150) 150g

Color 2: Green #430; 100 (100) 100g

Color 3: Clear Blue #437; 100 (100) 100g

Color 4: Orange Red #469; 50 (50) 50g

Color 5: Green #430; 50 (50) 50g

Color 6: Red #439; 50 (50) 50g

Note: For colorway 2, color 2 and color 5 are the same.

Gauge: 27 sts and 32 rows over pattern = 4 × 4 inches. Make a swatch to assure proper gauge.

Needle suggestion: Double-point and circular needles sizes 2 and 3 (2.5mm and 3mm), or size to obtain gauge.

Body: Using Dark Blue for both color-ways and smaller needle, cast on 144 (152) 160 sts. Join, being careful not to twist sts. Knit 7 rnds for facing, purl 1 rnd, and knit 1 rnd. Change to larger needle, and work Border 1. Before you go on to the next border, mark 3 sts on each side. Work the 3 side sts in color 1 on every rnd, and make the incs on each side of them. On the front, work Border 2, and on the back, work Border 3. Now start increasing 1 st on each side of the side sts—4 sts every rnd—as follows (start counting at the beginning of Borders 2/3): Size 1 year: Inc 4 sts after 9 rnds, then 4 sts every 9th rnd 4 times to 164 sts. Size 2 years: Inc 4 sts every 5th rnd 2 times, then 4 sts every 6th rnd 6 times to 184 sts. Size 3 years: Inc 4 sts after 6 rnds, then 4 sts every 5th rnd 9 times to 196 sts. When the body measures 6" (6¼") 6¼" from the purl rnd, bind off the 3 side sts on each side. On the next rnd, cast on 2 new sts over the bound-off sts. Purl the new sts every rnd using two strands. They are for machine stitching and cutting for sleeve openings later on. Work Borders 2/3 until you have made 10 (11) 12 rows of fishes. Then work Border 4. When the body measures 9¾" (11¾") 12½", bind off center front 23 (25) 25 sts for square neck opening. Keep working in the rnd, casting on 2 new sts over the bound-off sts. Purl the new sts every rnd using two strands. When the body measures 11⅜" (13⅜") 14⅛", bind off 23 (25) 25 sts for back square neck. On the next rnd, cast on 2 sts over the bound-off sts. Purl the new sts every rnd using two strands. Keep working in the rnd until full length. Bind off, or put the sts on holders.

Sleeves: Make 2. Using Dark Blue for both colorways and smaller needles, cast on 44 (56) 56 sts. Work 7 rnds for facing, purl 1

rnd, and knit 1 rnd. Change to larger needles and work Border 1. Three sts at underarm center are marking sts, and are worked in color 1 every rnd. Underarm incs are done on each side of these sts. Start working Border 3. After the 3rd rnd, inc 1 st on each side of the marking sts as follows: Size 1 year: Every other rnd 10 times, then every 3rd rnd 16 times. Size 2 years: Every other rnd 13 times, then every 3rd rnd 14 times. Size 3 years: Every other rnd 15 times, then every 3rd rnd 18 times. When the sleeve measures 7⅞" (9") 9¾", or at nearest complete repeat, work Border 4 for 8 rnds. Using

Dark Blue, purl 1 rnd, then knit 7 rnds for facing. Bind off. Make the other sleeve the same.

Finishing: For details on finishing, see Knitting Techniques on page 11. Using a sewing machine, zigzag 2 lines around the neck opening, one in the purl rnd, and the other in the rnd outside the purl. Cut open. Zigzag and cut the same way for sleeve openings. Graft or sew the shoulder seams. From the knit side, using Dark Blue and smaller needle, pick up sts around the neck. Knit 3 rnds, decreasing 1 st at each corner every rnd. Purl 1 rnd, then knit 5 rnds,

increasing 1 st at each corner every rnd. Sew in the sleeves. Weave all loose ends into the back of the fabric and sew the facings to the wrong side. Steam lightly on the wrong side.

Hat: The hat does not cover the ears. Check your gauge. A small difference in gauge can make a big difference in the finished size. Using Dark Blue and smaller needle, cast on 120 (124) 132 sts. Join, being careful not to twist sts. Knit 7 rnds for facing, purl 1 rnd, knit 3 rnds. Change to larger needle and work Border 4 according to the chart. Work one repeat of the zigzag design,

then vertical stripes. When the hat measures 2¼" (2¾") 3⅛ from the purl rnd, start decreasing. Divide the hat into 4 sections with 30 (31) 33 sts in each section. The first Blue st in each section (colorway 1: Dark Blue, colorway 2: Clear Blue) are marking sts. Dec 1 st on each side of the marking sts—8 sts every rnd—every 4th rnd 3 times, every 3rd rnd 2 times, then every other rnd until 4 Blue sts remain. Using Blue, knit 7 rnds over the 4 sts. Put remaining sts on yarn, gather, and fasten off. Sew the facing to the wrong side and steam the hat lightly.

BODY, front

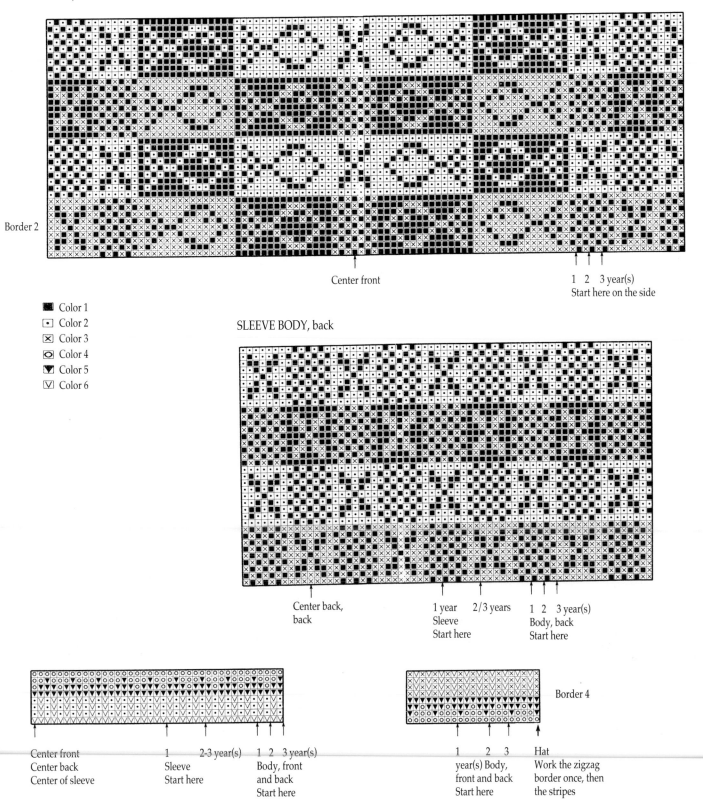

Border 2

Center front

1 2 3 year(s)
Start here on the side

☒ Color 1
☐ Color 2
☒ Color 3
☒ Color 4
☒ Color 5
☒ Color 6

SLEEVE BODY, back

Center back,
back

1 year
Sleeve
Start here

2/3 years

1 2 3 year(s)
Body, back
Start here

Border 4

Center front
Center back
Center of sleeve

1   2-3 year(s)
Sleeve
Start here

1 2 3 year(s)
Body, front
and back
Start here

1   2   3
year(s) Body,
front and back
Start here

Hat
Work the zigzag
border once, then
the stripes

Crazy About Cars

Sizes: 2 (4) 6 years

Finished Measurements:

Chest: 27½" (30⅝") 33⅞"

Length, pullover: 13¾" (16⅛") 16⅞"

Hips, pants: 11¾" (12⅛") 12½"

Head circumference: 18½" for all sizes

Yarn: Rauma Finullgarn

Blue #437; 400 (600) 800g

Red #439; 100 (100) 150g

Orange Red #469; 100 (100) 150g

Dark Yellow #450; 100 (100) 150g

Light Yellow #446; 100 (100) 150g

Medium Green #430; 100 (100) 150g

Light Green #493; 100 (100) 150g

Black #436; 50 (100) 100g

Gauge: 27 sts and 32 rows over pattern = 4 × 4 inches. Make a swatch to assure proper gauge.

Needle suggestion: Double-point and circular needles sizes 2 and 3 (2.5mm and 3mm), or size to obtain gauge.

Body: Using Black and smaller needle, cast on 150 (170) 190 sts. Join, being careful not to twist sts. Work k1, p1 ribbing for 1½". Change to larger needle and inc evenly spaced to 186 (209) 232 sts. The two center front sts are marking sts. Purl these sts every rnd using two strands (main and contrast color). They are to be machine stitched and cut open later on. Work Border 1 until the body measures 10¼" (13") 13¾". Now shape for neck and work back and forth. For details on working designs back and forth, see Knitting Techniques, "Neck opening", on page 00. Bind off center front 18 (20) 22 sts, including the center front purl sts. On the next row bind off 2 (2) 1 st on each side. Work even until the body measures 12½" (15⅜") 16⅛". Now bind off center back 36 (38) 40 sts for back neck and finish each side separately. Work even for 3/4" and finish after a complete car repeat. Bind off.

Sleeves: Make 2. Using Black and smaller needles, cast on 38 (40) 42 sts. Join, being careful not to twist sts. Work ribbing as for body. Change to larger needles and inc evenly spaced to 45 (49) 53 sts. Work Border 2, and *at the same time* inc 2 sts at underarm every 3rd rnd to 97 (113) 119 sts. Work until the sleeve measures 10⅝" (11¾") 13". Purl 6 rnds for facing, increasing 2 sts at underarm every rnd. Bind off.

Finishing: For details on finishing, see Knitting Techniques on page 11. Machine stitch and cut open at center front. Using Black, work k1, p1 ribbing, picking up sts along the front edges and working the front bands. Work ribbing for 1⅛" and bind off. On the buttonhole band, work ribbing for 1/2" first. Start at the top of the band and work as follows: Work 4 sts, *bind off 4 sts for buttonhole, work 10 sts*; repeat between *s across, ending with a buttonhole 4 sts from the lower edge. On the next row, cast on 4 sts over all the bound-off sts. Work for 1/2" and bind off. Machine stitch and cut for sleeve openings. Sew the shoulder seams. Using Black, pick up sts around the neck, starting and ending at the center of each

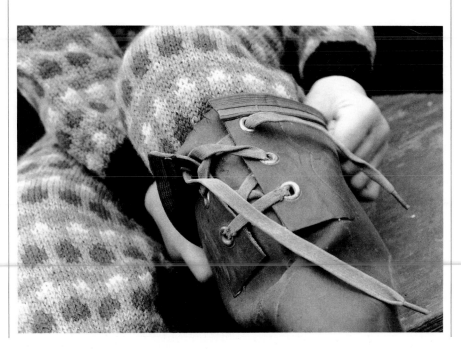

front band to make the collar meet at center front when the cardigan is buttoned up. Pick up the sts from the inside, and pick up enough sts at the curves to make the collar big enough. Work ribbing for 2¼" and bind off. Sew in the sleeves. Weave all loose ends into the back of the fabric, sew the facings to the wrong side, and steam lightly.

Pants: Using Black and smaller needle, cast on 46 (48) 50 sts. Join, being careful not to twist sts. Work k1, p1 ribbing for 1½". Change to larger needle and inc evenly spaced to 79 (89) 99 sts. Work Border 2, and *at the same time* inc 2 sts every 3rd rnd at the inseam to 109 (119) 129 sts. Work until the leg measures 11" (14⅛") 15¾". Now dec for the crotch and finish the leg working back and forth. Bind off 6 sts at the inseam, then 2 sts from each side every other row until you have decreased / bound off 14 (18) 22 sts from each side. Make another leg the same.

Joining the legs: Put the sts from both legs on one circular needle. Dec enough sts to make the pattern repeat come out even at the front and at the back of the pants. Work even until the pants measure 16⅞" (20⅞") 22⅜". Change to Black and smaller needle. Dec 20 sts evenly spaced and work ribbing for 1½". Now purl the knit sts and knit the purl sts for another 1½". Bind off. Sew the facing to the wrong side, sew in elastic, and sew the crotch seam. Weave all loose ends into the back of the fabric and steam lightly.

Hat: Check your gauge. A small difference in gauge can make a big difference in the finished size. Using Black and smaller needle, cast on 128 sts. Join, being careful not to twist sts. Knit facing for 1½". Purl 1 rnd, knit 2 rnds. Work 1 repeat of cars from Border 1. Work Border 2 until the hat measures 6¼" from the purl rnd. Put remaining sts on yarn, gather, and fasten off.

Ear flaps: Using Black, pick up 18 sts on the inside of the hat. Turn, and pick up another 18 sts going back to make the ear flap double, and join, being careful not to twist sts. Work for 1⅛". Start shaping as follows: *K3, dec 1*; repeat between *s around. Knit 3 rnds. *K2, dec 1*; repeat between *s around. Knit 2 rnds. *k1, dec 1*; repeat between *s around. Knit 1 rnd. K2tog around. Put remaining sts on yarn, gather,

and fasten off. Work the other ear flap the same. Sew the facing to the wrong side, weave all loose ends into the back of the fabric, and steam lightly. Make a small Black pompom and sew to the top of the hat. Optional: Make twisted cords and sew to the ear flaps.

Blue 437

■ Black 436

▼ Red 439

⊟ Orange Red 469

▲ Light Green 493

● Medium Green 430

⊠ Light Yellow 446

⊡ Dark Yellow 450

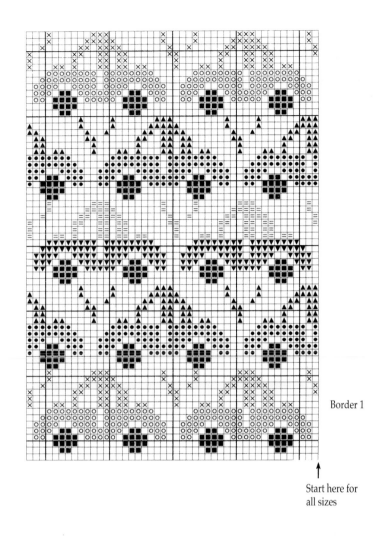

Border 1

Start here for
all sizes

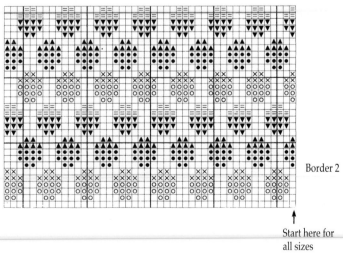

Border 2

Start here for
all sizes

Big Fishing Pullover

Sizes: 6 (9) 12 years

Finished Measurements:

Chest: 29⅞" (33") 37"

Length: 18⅛" (20") 22¾"

Head circumference: 17¾" (18½") 19⅝"

Yarn: Rauma Finullgarn

Colorway 1—Brown pullover:

Color 1: Brown #464; 250 (300) 350g

Color 2: Violet #474; 50 (50) 50g

Color 3: Purple #496; 50 (50) 50g

Color 4: Blue #467; 50 (50) 50g

Color 5: Green #421; 50 (50) 50g

Color 6: Clear Blue #437; 50 (50) 50g

Color 7: Light Green #483; 50 (50) 50g

Colorway 2—Blue pullover:

Color 1: Dark Blue #482; 250 (300) 350g

Color 2: Red #439; 50 (50) 50g

Color 3: Orange Red #469; 50 (50) 50g

Color 4: Blue #467; 50 (50) 50g

Color 5: Green #421; 50 (50) 50g

Color 6: Clear Blue #437; 50 (50) 50g

Color 7: Grass Green #430; 50 (50) 50g

Gauge: 27 sts and 32 rows over pattern = 4 × 4 inches. Make a swatch to assure proper gauge.

Needle suggestion: Double-point and circular needles sizes 2 and 3 (2.5mm and 3mm), or size to obtain gauge.

Note: In the fish design it is important to catch the yarn in the back to avoid long strands. Keep the thread you are working with towards the tip of your left index finger, and place the other thread inside it on the same finger. With your right needle, go under the inner thread to knit the outer thread, then go over the inner thread to knit the outer thread. Repeat this procedure once to several times, depending on how far you have to carry the yarn.

Body: Using color 1 and smaller needle, cast on 176 (192) 216 sts. Join, being careful not to twist sts. Knit 7 rnds for facing, purl 1 rnd, and knit 6 rnds. Make 3 sts on each side marking sts. Work the marking sts in color 1 every rnd, and make the incs on each side of them. Change to larger needle and start Border 1. Inc 1 st on each side of the marking sts—4 incs each rnd—as follows (start counting number of rnds before the first inc at the beginning of Border 1): Size 6 years: Inc 4 sts after the 6th rnd, then 4 sts every 6th rnd 7 times, to 208 sts. Size 9 years: Inc 4 sts after the 7th rnd, then 4 sts every 6th rnd 6 times, and 4 sts every 7th rnd 2 times, to 228 sts. Size 12 years: Inc 4 sts after the 7th rnd, then 4 sts every 7th rnd 8 times, to 256 sts. Work until the body measures 8¾" (8¾") 11⅜" from the beginning of Border 1. Bind off the 3 marking sts on each side. Cast on 2 sts over the bound-off sts on the next rnd. Purl the new sts every rnd using two strands. They are for machine stitching and cutting later on. Work 5 (6) 7 repeats of fish before starting Border 2. When the body measures 16" (17¾") 20" from the beginning of Border 1, bind off center front 31 (31) 35 sts for square neck. On the next rnd, cast on 2 sts over the bound-off sts, and keep working in the rnd. Purl the new sts every rnd using two strands. They will be machine stitched and cut later on. When the body measures 17¼" (19¼") 22" from the beginning of Border 1, bind off center back 31 (31) 35 sts for back neck. On the next rnd, cast on 2 new sts over the bound-off sts, and keep working in the rnd. Purl the new sts every rnd using two strands. Bind off, or put the sts on holders when the body measures full length from the beginning of Border 1.

Sleeves: Make 2. Using color 1 and smaller needles, cast on 60 (66) 68 sts. Join, being careful not to twist sts. Knit 7 rnds for facing, purl 1 rnd, and knit 7 rnds. Make the 3 center underarm sts marking sts. Work the marking sts in color 1 every rnd and make all the incs on each side of these sts. Change to larger needles and work Border 1. After the 4th rnd of Border 1, start increasing 1 st on each side of the marking sts as follows: Size 6 years: Inc 2 sts every 3rd rnd 34 times. Size 9 years: Inc 2 sts every 3rd rnd 34 times, then 2 sts every 4th rnd 4 times. Size 12 years: Inc 2 sts every 3rd rnd 39 times, then 2 sts every 4th rnd 6 times. Work 4 (5) 6 repeats of fish before starting Border 2. Work Border 2 until the sleeve measures 13¾" (15¾") 18½", or finish with a complete repeat if you are at full length and are just a couple rnds short. Purl 1 rnd, then knit 7 rnds for facing. Bind off.

Finishing: For details on finishing, see Knitting Techniques on page 11. Machine stitch two zigzag lines around the neck; one in the purl rnd, the other in the next rnd to the outside. Cut open. Machine stitch around the arm openings the same way, and cut open. Sew or graft the shoulders together. With the right side facing, using Dark Blue and smaller needles, pick up sts around the neck. Knit 3 rnds, decreasing 1 st at each corner every rnd. Purl 1 rnd, then knit 5 rnds, increasing 1 st at each corner every rnd for facing. Sew in the sleeves. Weave all loose ends into the back of the fabric, sew the facings to the wrong side, and steam lightly.

Hat: Check your gauge. A small difference in gauge can make a big difference in the finished size. Using color 1 and smaller needles, cast on 120 (128) 136 sts. Join, being careful not to twist sts. Knit 7 rnds for facing, purl 1 rnd, then knit 3 rnds. Change to larger needle and work the first repeat of Border 1 (29 rnds). Change to smaller needles. The rest of the hat is worked in color 1 only. Knit 6 rnds. Start decreasing in the next rnd as follows: *K6, k2tog*; repeat between *s around. Knit 5 rnds. *K5, k2tog*; repeat between *s around. Continue decreasing like this with 1 rnd less between dec rnds, and 1 st less between decs until 1 st between decs (k1, k2tog). Knit 1 rnd. Put remaining sts on yarn, gather, and fasten off. Sew the facing to the wrong side. Using color 4, make a small pompom and sew to the top of the hat.

MODEL 25

Alternative 1:

☐ Color 1: Brown 464
☒ Color 2: Violet 474
• Color 3: Purple 496
● Color 4: Blue 467
☐ Color 5: Green 421
Ⓞ Color 6: Clear Blue 437
– Color 7: Light Green 483

Alternative 2:

☐ Dark Blue 482
☒ Red 439
• Orange Red 469
● Blue 467
☐ Green 421
Ⓞ Clear Blue 437
– Grass Green 430

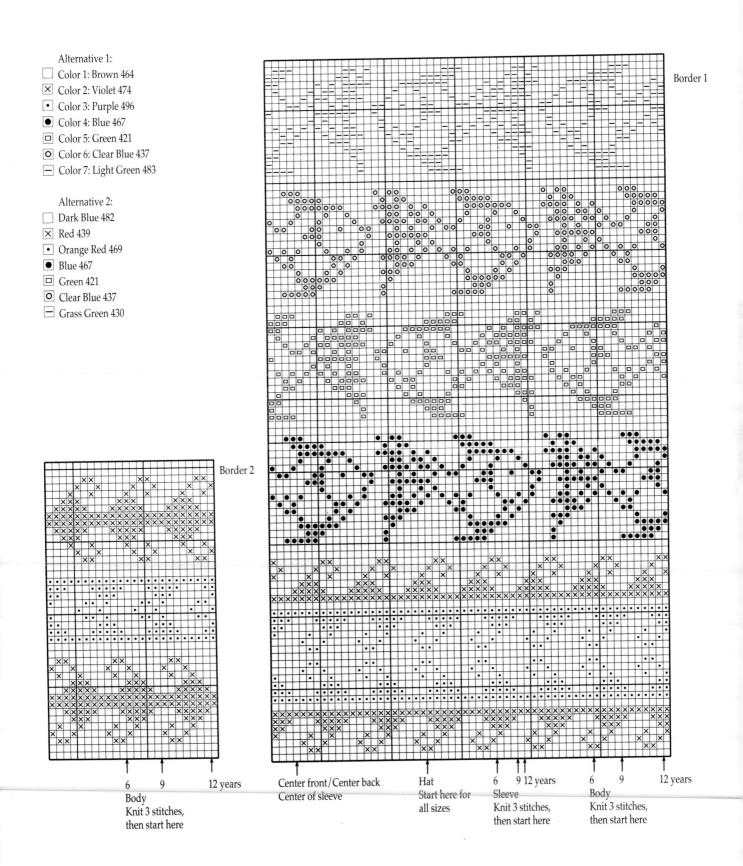

Border 1

Border 2

6   9   12 years

Body
Knit 3 stitches,
then start here

Center front / Center back
Center of sleeve

Hat
Start here for
all sizes

6   9 12 years
Sleeve
Knit 3 stitches,
then start here

6   9   12 years
Body
Knit 3 stitches,
then start here

119

Birds of Paradise

Sizes: 6 (8) 10 (12) 14 years

Finished Measurements:

Chest: 33" (36¼") 38½" (40⅞") 44"

Length, pullover: 18⅛" (19⅝") 20⅜" (22") 24⅜"

Length, stockings: 15¾" (15¾") 19⅝" (23⅝") 23⅝"

Head circumference: 20⅜" (20⅜") (22") 22"

Yarn: Rauma Finullgarn

Pullover:

Dark Green #484; 100 (100) 150 (150) 200g

Medium Green #430; 100 (150) 150 (200) 200g

Light Green #493; 100 (100) 150 (150) 200g

Turquoise #483; 100 (150) 150 (200) 200g

Yellow #450; 50 (50) 50 (50) 50g

Orange #469; 50 (50) 50 (50) 50g

Red #439; 200 (200) 250 (300) 300g

Rose #4886; 50 (50) 50 (50) 50g

Stockings 6/8 (10/12) 14 years:

Dark Green #484; 50 (50) 100g

Medium Green #430; 50 (50) 100g

Light Green #493; 50 (50) 100g

Turquoise #483; 50 (50) 100g

Yellow #450; 50 (50) 50g

Orange #469; 50 (50) 50g

Red #439; 100 (100) 100g

Rose #4886; 50 (50) 50g

Black, "Gammel Serie"; 50 (50) 50g

Gauge: 27 sts and 32 rows over pattern = 4 × 4 inches. Make a swatch to assure proper gauge.

Needle suggestion: Double-point and circular needles size 2 and 3 (2.5mm and 3mm), or size to obtain gauge.

Body: Using Red and smaller needle, cast on 190 (210) 230 (250) 270 sts. Join, being careful not to twist sts. Knit 1½" for facing. Make a picot edge: *Yarn over, k2tog*; repeat between *s around. Knit 2 rnds. Work Border 1. Change to larger needle and work Border 2. All the borders will not come out even at the sides, so it will look better if you make a one-colored vertical stripe on each side. Work Borders 3, 4, 5, 6, 3, 2, 7, 4, 5, 6, 3, 2 according to the chart, and *at the same time* inc 2 sts on each side every 4th rnd to 226 (246) 266 (280) 300 sts. Work until the body measures 14½" (16⅛") 16⅞" (18½") 20⅞" from the picot edge. Bind off center front 36 (38) 38 (38) 38 sts. On the next rnd, cast on 2 sts over the bound-off sts. Purl the new sts every rnd using two strands. They are for machine stitching and cutting later on. Knit in the rnd for 2¾". Now bind off center back 36 (38) 38 (38) 38 sts. Work back and forth for 3/4". For details on working designs back and forth, see Knitting Techniques, "Neck opening", on page 11. Bind off remaining sts, or put them on holders.

Sleeves: Make 2. Using Red and smaller needles, cast on 43 (45) 47 (49) 49 sts. Join, being careful not to twist sts. Knit 1½" for facing. Make a picot edge: *Yarn over, k2tog*; repeat between *s around. Work Border 1 as for body. Change to larger needles, increasing evenly spaced to 51 (53) 55 (57) 59 sts. Work borders as the body, and inc 2 sts at underarm every 3rd rnd to 119 (125) 135 (145) 157 sts. Work until the sleeve measures 13¾" (14½") 15¾" (17¾") 19¼" from the picot edge. Finish with a complete border. Purl 6 rnds for facing, increasing 2 sts at underarm every rnd. Bind off.

Finishing: For details on finishing, see Knitting Techniques on page 11. Machine stitch and cut open for the sleeves. Sew or graft the shoulders together. Using Red and smaller needles, pick up sts around the neck. Knit 2 rnds, then make a picot edge: *Yarn over, k2tog*; repeat between *s around. Knit 6 rnds, increasing 2 sts at each corner every rnd. Bind off. Sew in the sleeves. Weave all loose ends into the back of the fabric, and sew the facings to the wrong side. Steam lightly.

Square Hat with Long Tail: 6/8/10 (12/14) years. Check your gauge. A small difference in gauge can make a big difference in the finished size. Using Red and smaller needle, cast on 140 (150) sts. Join, being careful not to twist sts. Work the facing and Border 1 as for the body. Change to larger needle and work Border 2. Then work Border 3, placing a marker at 35 (40), 70 (80), 105 (120), and 140 (160) sts. Start increasing 1 st on each side of the markers at the beginning of Border 3. Inc every rnd 20 times, and then work 2 rnds of Red. Now make the top of the hat. Put the sts between the markers on 4 needles. Work sts 1 to 35 (40) back and forth, but every time you turn,

knit the last st together with 2 sts from needle 2 and needle 4 (k3tog). Work Borders 4, 5, 2, and 3 until the sts from only needle 1 and needle 3 remain. Now make the long tip of the hat. From now on, dec on each side. Using the main color of the border, dec 1 st on each side of the center st. Work Borders 6, 3, and 2. *At the same time,* dec 2 sts on each side every other rnd. Knit and dec until approximately 16 sts remain. Using one color only, work until 4 sts remain. Put remaining sts on yarn and fasten off. Sew the facing to the wrong side and sew a pompom to the top of the hat.

Stockings: 6–8 (10–12) 14 years. Make 2. Using Red and smaller needles, cast on 68 (74) 78 sts. Join, being careful not to twist sts. Work k2, p2 ribbing in a stripe design: *Medium Green 3 rnds, Rose 2 rnds, Light Green 5 rnds, Yellow 2 rnds, Orange 4 rnds, Dark Green 2 rnds, Red 6 rnds, Turquoise 4 rnds, Yellow 2 rnds*; repeat between *s until the stocking measures 5⅞" (9¾") 13¾". Continue knitting the stripe design, and start decreasing 2 sts at center back every 6th rnd until 44 (48) 48 sts remain. Work until the stocking measures 13¾" (17¾") 21⅝". Change to Black, "Gammel Serie" (a more durable yarn). Work the heel over the sts on needle 1 and needle 4—22 (24) 24 sts. Always slip the first st on the needle without knitting. Work back and forth for approximately 2" (2") 2", finishing with a knit row.

Turning the heel: Purl until 2 sts beyond the center, p2tog, p1. Turn. Knit until 2 sts beyond the center, sl 1, k1, psso, k1. Turn. Purl until the st before the "hole". Purl the st before the hole and the st after the hole together, p1. Turn. Knit until the st before the hole. Sl 1, k1, psso. Turn. Continue work-

ing like this until all the sts outside the hole are decreased. Pick up 8 (10) 10 sts on each side of the heel flap and knit in the rnd. Dec 1 st on each side every 4th rnd until 40 (42) 42 sts are on the needles. Work until the foot measures approximately 5½" (6¼") 7".

Shaping the toe: Dec 2 sts on each side of the foot. Knit 3 rnds, and dec 2 sts on each side. Knit 3 rnds, then dec 2 sts on each side until 8 sts remain. Put remaining sts on yarn, gather, and fasten off.

MODEL 26

- ■ Red 439
- ⊡ Yellow 450
- ⊡ Medium Green 430
- ◎ Rose 4886
- ▣ Turquoise 483
- ▼ Orange 469
- ⊞ Dark Green 484
- ▨ Light Green 493

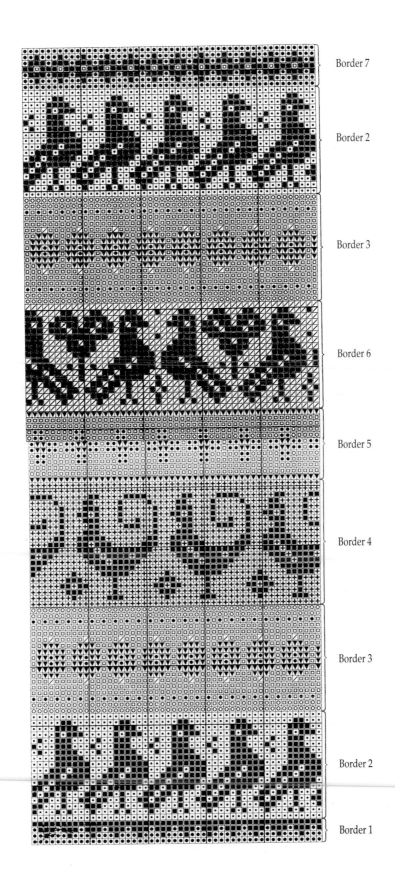

Border 7

Border 2

Border 3

Border 6

Border 5

Border 4

Border 3

Border 2

Border 1

MODEL 27

Ocean Glow Pullover

Sizes: 6 (8) 10 (12) 14 years

Finished Measurements:

Chest: 32¼" (34⅝") 37¾" (40⅞") 44"

Length: 18⅛" (19⅝") 20⅜" (22") 24⅜"

Head circumference: 20⅜" (20⅜") 20⅜" (23¼") 23¼"

Yarn: Rauma Finullgarn

Blue #437; 50 (50) 50 (50) 100g

Yellow #450; 50 (50) 50 (50) 50g

Red #439; 50 (50) 50 (50) 50g

Rose #4886; 50 (50) 50 (50) 50g

Turquoise #483; 200 (250) 250 (300) 300g

Green #485; 200 (250) 250 (300) 300g

Gauge: 27 sts and 32 rows over pattern = 4 × 4 sts. Make a swatch to assure proper gauge.

Needle suggestion: Double-point and circular needles sizes 2 and 3 (2.5mm and 3mm), or size to obtain gauge.

Body: Using Turquoise and smaller needle, cast on 200 (220) 240 (260) 280 sts. Join, being careful not to twist sts. Knit 2¼" for facing, then work a picot edge: *Yarn over, k2tog*; repeat between *s around. Knit 2 rnds, then work Border 1. Change to larger needle and inc evenly spaced to 220 (240) 260 (280) 300 sts. Work Border 2. The medallion repeat takes 40 sts at center front and center back. Duplicate stitch the color details later. Work the Main design over remaining sts. Work until the body measures 3 (3½) 4 (4)

4½ medallions. Bind off center front 36 (36) 38 (38) 38 sts for front neck. On the next rnd, cast on 2 sts over the bound-off sts. Purl the new sts every rnd using two strands. Work another 1/2 medallion. Bind off center back 36 (36) 38 (38) 38 sts. Work back and forth for 3/4". For details on working design back and forth, see Knitting Technique, "Neck opening", on page 11. Bind off or put the sts on holders.

Sleeves: Make 2. Using Turquoise and smaller needles, cast on 40 (46) 46 (48) 48 sts. Join, being careful not to twist sts. Work facing, picot edge, and Border 1 as for the body. Change to Turquoise and larger needles, and inc evenly spaced to 47 (53) 55 (57) 59 sts. Work the Main design without the medallion, and *at the same time* inc 2 sts at underarm every 3rd rnd until 119 (125) 135 (145) 155 sts. Work until the sleeve measures 13¾" (14½") 16⅛" (18½") 19¼" from the "picot edge". Purl 6 rnds for facing, increasing 2 sts at underarm every rnd. Bind off.

Finishing: For details on finishing, see Knitting Techniques on page 11. Machine stitch and cut open for sleeves and neck. Graft or sew the shoulders together. Using Yellow, pick up sts around the neck. Knit 2 rnds, then picot edge: *Yarn over, k2tog*; repeat between *s around. Knit 8 rnds, increasing 2 sts at each corner. Bind off and sew the facing to the wrong side. Sew in the sleeves and duplicate st the color details on the medallions. Weave all loose ends into the back of the fabric. Sew the facings to the wrong side. Steam lightly.

Hat with Earflaps: 6/8/10 (12/14) years. Check your gauge. A small difference in gauge can make a big difference in the finished size. Using Turquoise and smaller

needle, cast on 140 (160) sts. Join, being careful not to twist sts. Work facing, picot edge, and Border 1 as for the body. Change to larger needle and work the Main design without the medallion until the hat measures 6⅝" (7") from the picot edge. Put remaining sts on yarn, gather, and fasten off.

Earflaps: From the inside of the hat, using Blue, pick up 20 sts, turn, and pick up 20 sts going back (to make the earflap double). Join, being careful not to twist sts. Knit for 1⅛". Start the decreasing: *K3, dec 1*; repeat between *s around. Knit 3 rnds. *K2, dec 1*; repeat between *s around. Knit 2 rnds. *K1, dec 1*; repeat between *s around. Knit 1 rnd. K2tog around. Put remaining sts on yarn and gather. Make the other earflap. Weave all loose ends into the back of the fabric. Sew the facings to the wrong side. Steam lightly. Duplicate stitch the details on the hat, make a small Red pompom, and sew it to the top.

☐ Turquoise 483

■ Green 485

◉ Red 439

◙ Yellow 450

⊡ Blue 437

▣ Rose 4886

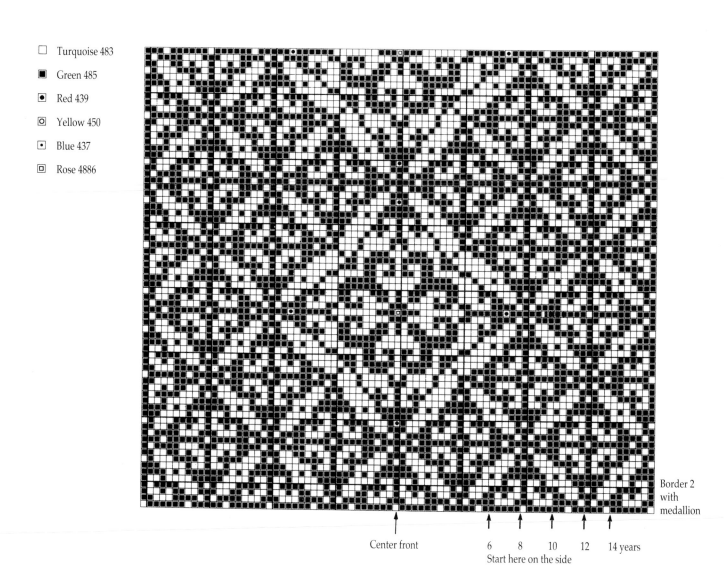

Border 2
with
medallion

Center front

6   8   10   12   14 years

Start here on the side

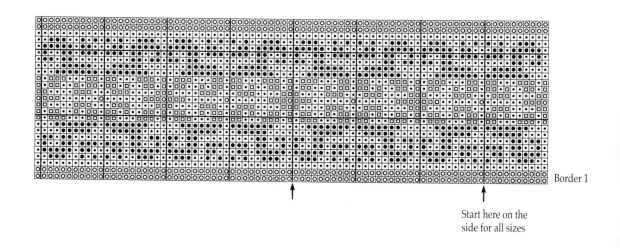

Border 1

Start here on the
side for all sizes

Border 3

Elephant Cardigan

Sizes: 8 (10) 12 years

Finished Measurements:

Chest: 35⅜" (37¾") 40⅞"

Length: 19⅝" (22¾") 26"

Head circumference: 20" (21¼") 21¼"

Yarn: Rauma Finullgarn

Rose #4886; 150 (200) 200g

Dark Blue #459; 300 (350) 350g

Sky Blue #437; 50 (50) 50g

Yellow #446; 50 (50) 50g

Green #4887; 50 (50) 50g

Gauge: 27 sts and 32 rows over pattern = 4 × 4 sts. Make a swatch to assure proper gauge.

Needle suggestion: Double-point and circular sizes 2 and 3 (2.5mm and 3mm), or size necessary to obtain gauge.

Body: Using Sky Blue and smaller needle, cast on 198 (219) 240 sts. Join, being careful not to twist sts. Make the 2 center front sts the marking sts. Purl these sts every rnd using two strands. They are for machine stitching and cutting later on. Knit 1⅛" for facing, purl 1 rnd, knit 2 rnds. Work Border 1. Change to larger needle and start Border 2. The cardigan has elephants on each side of the front opening, and the Main design on the sides and on the back. Make 1 st on each side a marking st. Knit these marking sts in one color, and inc 1 st on each side of them every 4th rnd (4 sts increased each inc rnd) to 242 (259) 280 sts. Work until the body measures 5 (6) 7 elephants. Bind off center front 32 (34) 36 sts for front neck, but keep purling the 2 center front marking sts so you can knit in the rnd. Work for 2". Bind off center back 32 (34) 36 sts. Finish the last elephant, bind off, or put remaining sts on holders.

Sleeves: Make 2. Using Sky Blue and smaller needles, cast on 40 (42) 44 sts. Join, being careful not to twist sts. Work the facing and Border 1 in the rnd as for the body. Change to larger needles, and inc evenly spaced to 47 (49) 51 sts. Work the Main design of Border 2, and *at the same time* inc 2 sts at underarm every 3rd rnd to 125 (135) 145 sts. Work until the sleeve measures 14⅛" (15¾") 17¾". Purl 6 rnds for facing, increasing 2 sts at underarm every rnd. Bind off.

Finishing: For details on finishing, see Knitting Techniques on page 11. Machine stitch and cut for front opening. Using Yellow, pick up sts along the front edges. To be able to knit the front edging in the rnd, cast on 2 extra sts at the top and at the bottom. Purl these sts every rnd. They will be machine stitched and cut later on. Work Border 1. Using Sky Blue, knit 1 rnd, purl 1 rnd, then knit 6 rnds for facing. Bind off. Machine stitch and cut for sleeve openings. Graft or sew the shoulders together. Using Sky Blue, pick up sts around the neck. Knit 1 rnd, purl 1 rnd. Knit 8 rnds, increasing 2 sts at each

corner every rnd. Bind off and sew the facing to the wrong side. Sew in the sleeves. Weave all loose ends into the back of the fabric and sew remaining facings to the wrong side. Steam lightly. Optional: Sew small glass beads in the body of the elephants.

Hat: 8 (10/12) years. Check your gauge. A small difference in gauge can make a big difference in the finished size. Using Sky Blue and larger needle, cast on 133 (140) sts. Join, being careful not to twist sts. Work facing and Border 1 as for the body. Increase evenly spaced to 136 (143) sts. Now work elephants according to the hat chart: 2 elephants facing each other over center front 63 sts, and the Main design over remaining 73 (80) sts. Between the elephants and the Main design, work a one-colored st every rnd as the sides of the body. Finish the elephant border. Using Rose, knit 2 rnds. Change to Dark Blue, purl 2 rnds, then knit, decreasing as follows: *Dec 1, k6*; repeat between *s around. Knit 5 rnds even. *Dec 1, k5*; repeat between *s around. Knit 5 rnds even. *Dec 1, k4*; repeat between *s around. Knit 10 rnds even. *Dec 1, k4*; repeat between *s around. Knit 10 rnds even. *Dec 1, k3*; repeat between *s around. Knit 15 rnds even. *Dec 1, k2 sts*; repeat between *s around. Knit 15 rnds even. *Dec 1, k1*; repeat between *s around. Knit 15 rnds even. K2tog around. Knit 15 rnds even. Put remaining sts on yarn and gather. Weave all loose ends into the back of the fabric and sew the facing to the wrong side. Using the tip of the hat, tie a knot at the top.

☐	Rose 4886
⊡	Sky Blue 437
☒	Yellow 446
■	Dark Blue 459
▪	Green 4887

Left front border   Right front border   (The front border is worked at the time of finishing)

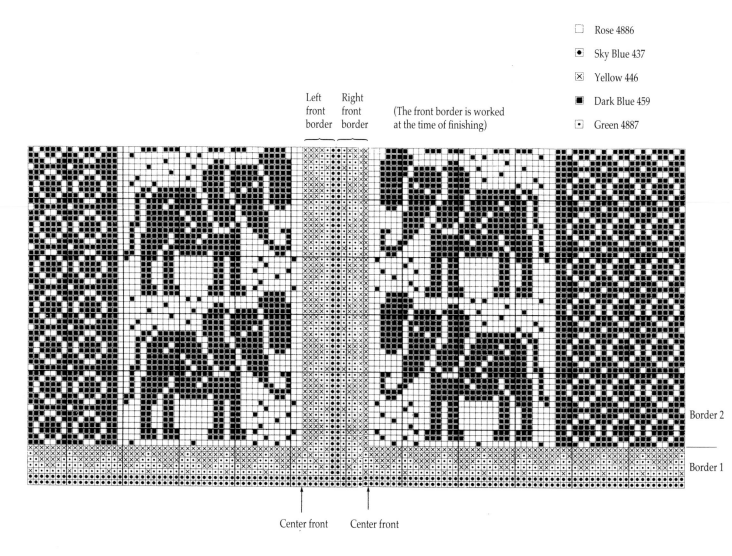

Border 2

Border 1

Center front   Center front

HAT

Border 2

Border 1

Mittens, Hats, Stockings, and Socks

Traditional ski stockings, mittens, and hats are both
practical and decorative. In addition, they are fun to make.
A pair of mittens or a hat with a star on the top can be finished
in a few evenings. Ski stockings will probably take a little longer.
The mittens and hat charts look like the shape of mittens and hats.
There is one design for each size. Making them may remind you
of a crossword or jigsaw puzzle. Don't be afraid to try these,
even if you have never made patterned mittens or hats before.
Because the design is made specially for the shape,
you will see at once if you make a mistake. Just make sure
you start out with the right number of stitches.
The ski stockings in this book have designs that can be
made up in different sizes. You will also find directions on how to fit
your own design into the basic pattern.

Warm Mittens with Stars

Here you'll find nine different mitten patterns. Some of them are related to the star designs on the ski stockings and hats, so you can make a set of hats, mittens, and ski stockings. You don't need a lot of yarn for mittens, so leftovers can be used. Traditionally, the mittens were made in Natural and one other color, which would make the design stand out. But the mittens are nice in other colors also, as long as the contrast is strong. When you make mittens, it is very important not to carry long strands on the wrong side. It is quite irritating if your fingers get caught in strands. If you have to carry the yarn more than 3 to 5 stitches, make sure to catch it in the back. For example, keep the thread you are working with towards the tip of your left index finger, and place the other thread inside it on the same finger. With your right needle, go under the inner thread to knit the outer thread, then go over the inner thread to knit the outer thread. Repeat this procedure once or several times, depending on how far you have to carry the yarn.

The basic pattern for these mittens are from Rauma's mitten collection, but the designs themselves are made for this book.

Sizes: 3/5 (7/9) 12/14 years

Yarn: Rauma Strikkegarn

Contrast color: 50 (50) 100g

Main color: 50 (50) 50g

Mitten 1: Red #174 and White #101

Mitten 2: Rose #7/71 and Rose #5/71

Mitten 3: Blue #149 and White #101

Mitten 4: Blue #159 and Green #145

Mitten 5: Blue #143 and White #101

Mitten 6: Charcoal #116 and White #101

Mitten 7: Green #130 and White #101

Mitten 8: Violet #112 and Rose #5/71

Mitten 9: Black #136 and White #101

The contrast color is listed first = marked square on the chart.

Gauge: 24 sts and 28 rows over pattern = 4 × 4 inches. Make a swatch to assure proper gauge.

Needle suggestion: Double-point needles sizes 2 and 3 (2.5mm and 3mm). If you knit tightly, use size 3 (3mm) for the ribbing, and 4 (3.5mm) for the hand, or size to obtain gauge.

Left Mitten: Using contrast color and smaller needles, cast on 32 (36) 40 sts. Join, being careful not to twist sts. Work k2, p2 ribbing for 2¼" (2¾") 3⅛". Change to larger needles, and knit 1 rnd, increasing evenly spaced to 34 (38) 42 sts. Start working the design and inc for the gusset according to the chart. At X on the chart, k9 using a piece of scrap yarn. Work them over again according to the chart as the chart indicates above the line by X. (When making the thumb, remove the scrap yarn, and knit the thumb over the sts then revealed). Keep working the design, and dec according to the chart. Decreasing: At the beginning of needles 1 and 3, sl 1, k1, psso. At the end of needles 2 and 4, k2tog. Dec until 8 sts are on the needles. Put remaining sts on yarn and gather. Weave all loose ends into the back of the fabric.

Thumb: Remove the scrap yarn you knitted the 9 thumb sts onto. Now you have 17 sts. Pick up 2 (2) 3 sts on one side and 1 (1) 2 sts on the other side of the thumb—20 (20) 22 are on the needles. Using larger needles, work according to the chart and dec as for the mitten.

Make the right mitten the same, but inc for the gusset at the beginning of the palm sts, rather than at the end.

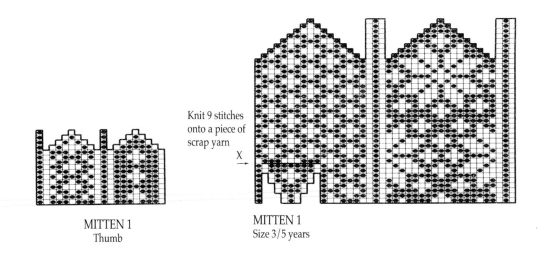

Knit 9 stitches
onto a piece of
scrap yarn

X →

MITTEN 1
Thumb

MITTEN 1
Size 3/5 years

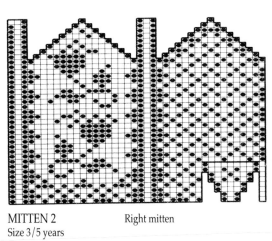

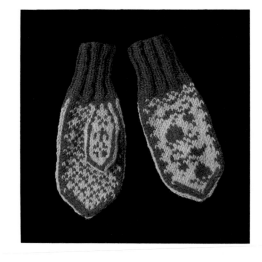

X ←

Knit 9 stitches
onto a piece of
scrap yarn

MITTEN 2
Size 3/5 years

Right mitten

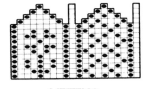

MITTEN 2
Right thumb

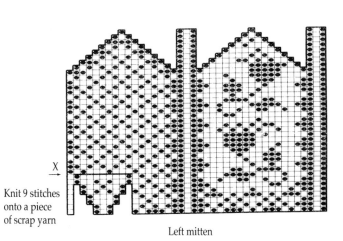

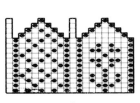

X →

Knit 9 stitches
onto a piece
of scrap yarn

Left thumb

Left mitten

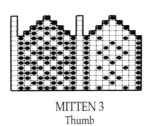

Knit 9 stitches onto a piece of scrap yarn

X →

MITTEN 3
Size 3/5 years

MITTEN 3
Thumb

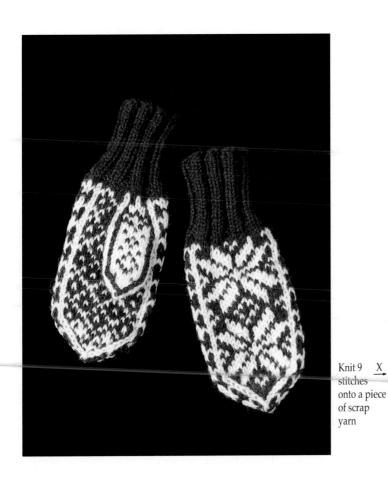

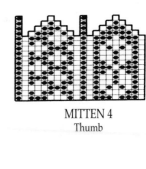

MITTEN 4
Thumb

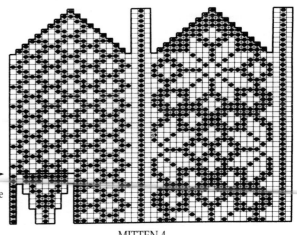

Knit 9 stitches onto a piece of scrap yarn

X →

MITTEN 4
Size 7/9 years

137

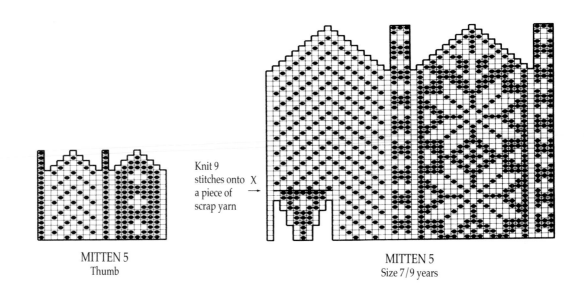

Knit 9
stitches onto
a piece of
scrap yarn → X

MITTEN 5
Thumb

MITTEN 5
Size 7/9 years

MITTEN 6
Thumb

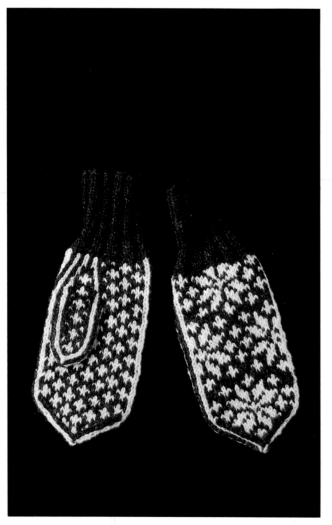

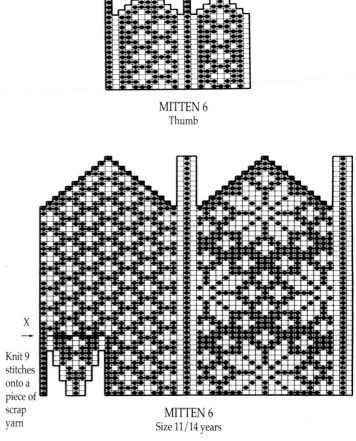

X
→

Knit 9
stitches
onto a
piece of
scrap
yarn

MITTEN 6
Size 11/14 years

138

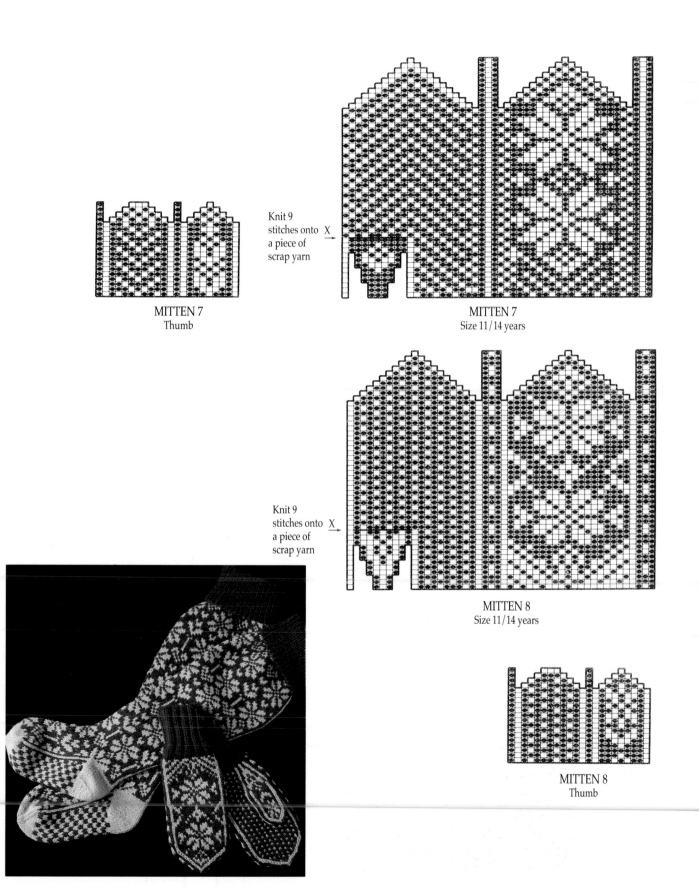

MITTEN 7
Thumb

Knit 9
stitches onto
a piece of
scrap yarn   X

MITTEN 7
Size 11/14 years

Knit 9
stitches onto
a piece of
scrap yarn   X

MITTEN 8
Size 11/14 years

MITTEN 8
Thumb

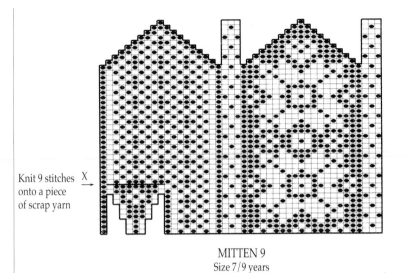

Knit 9 stitches onto a piece of scrap yarn X →

MITTEN 9
Size 7/9 years

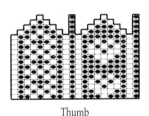

Thumb

Small Hat with Stars

This little hat matches many of the mitten patterns, and two of the ski stocking patterns. Use the same colors for the mittens, ski stockings, and the hat to make a set.

Sizes: 3/5 (7/9) 11/14 years
Finished measurements:
   Head circumference: 17 3/4" (18 1/2") 19 5/8"
Yarn: Rauma Strikkegarn
   Contrast color: 50 (50) 50g
   Main color: 50 (50) 50g
Color suggestions:
   Design 1: Red #174 and White #101
   Design 2: Blue #143 and White #101
   Design 3: Green #130 and White #101
(The contrast color is listed first = marked square on the chart.)
Gauge: 24 sts and 28 rows over pattern = 4 × 4 sts. Make a swatch to assure proper gauge.
Needle suggestion: Double-point needles size 3 (3mm), short circular needle sizes 2 and 3 (2.5mm and 3mm), or size to obtain gauge.

Using Main color and smaller needles, cast on 108 (114) 120 sts. Join, being careful not to twist sts. Knit 9 rnds, then purl 1 rnd. Now work the design according to the chart, but change to larger needles after 2 rnds of main color. (Note that in some rnds in the design you have to carry the contrast color over many sts. Make sure you catch it in the

back if you have to carry over more than 5 or
6 sts to avoid long strands.) Dec as indicated
on the chart. Put remaining sts on yarn and
gather. Sew the facing to the wrong side.
Weave all loose ends into the back of the
fabric. Optional: Make a pompom and sew
to the top.

HAT 1
Size 3/5 years
The graph shows half of the hat

HAT 2
Size 7/9 years
The graph shows half of the hat

HAT 3
Size 11/14 years
The graph shows half of the hat

1.

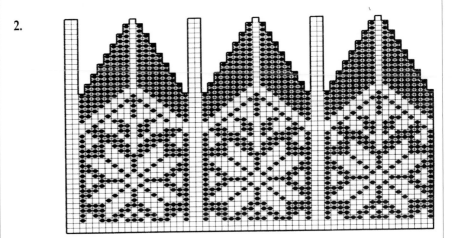

2.

3.

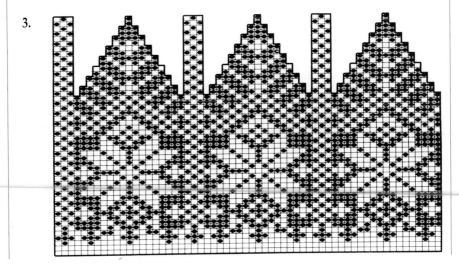

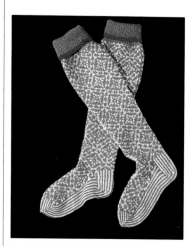

The patterns for these
ski stockings are found
on page 72.

Ski Stockings with Stars

This stocking pattern is from Rauma
Ullvarefabrikk's stocking collection, but the
design is made for this book.

Sizes: 3/5 (7/9) 12/14 years
Yarn: Rauma Strikkegarn
    Contrast color: 100 (150) 150g
    Main color: 100 (100) 100g
    Design 1: Black #136 and White #101
    Design 2: Red #174 and White #101
    Design 3: Violet #112 and Rose #5/71
    Design 4: Green #130 and White #101
You can also make the stockings in one
    color, or make up your own design. On
    the chart, the marked square is the con-
    trast color, the open square is the main
    color.
Gauge: 24 sts and 28 rows over pattern = 4 ×
    4 sts. Make a swatch to assure proper
    gauge.
Needle suggestion: Double-point needles
    sizes 2 and 3 (2.5mm and 3mm) if you are
    doing stockings with a design. Use nee-
    dles size 2 (2.5mm) all the time if you are
    making solid-colored stockings (you may
    do embroidery on solid-color stockings).
    If you knit tightly, use needles size 3
    (3mm) for the ribbing and solid-colored
    stockinette stitch, and 4 (3.5mm) for two-
    color knitting. Stockings should be knit a

little tighter than other garments for durability.

Using contrast color and smaller needles, cast on 52 (60) 68 sts. Join, being careful not to twist sts. Work ribbing in the rnd for 3⅛" (4") 4¾". Knit 1 rnd, increasing evenly spaced to 60 (68) 78 sts. If you are working a two-color design, change to larger needles. The first 3 sts on the rnd are worked as follows: Contrast color 1 st, main color 1 st, and contrast color 1 st. Work these stripes at the beginning of the first needle all the way down to the heel. All the dec for the leg are done on each side of these 3 sts. (Also on solid-colored stockings it looks best if you dec on each side of the 3 center back sts.) The arrows on the chart show where to start for each size. After 2¼" (3⅛") 4", dec 1 st on each side of the 3 (striped) center back sts every 6th (6th) 5th rnd until 46 (50) 54 sts remain. Work until the stocking measures 13" (15¾") 18½". Now distribute the sts so you have the same number on each needle. Make sure that the 3 center back (striped) sts end up the center of the heel when you put all the sts from needle 1 and needle 4—23

(25) 27—onto one needle to make the heel. Work the heel using only the contrast or only the main color. Work stockinette stitch back and forth over the heel sts for 12 (14) 16 rows, ending with a knit row. Slip the first st on each row without knitting. If you find it hard to get an even gauge going back and forth, try working the purl rows on one size smaller needles (for example; use needles size 1 (2.5mm) if you are using size 2 (3mm) for the knit rows).

Turning the heel: Mark the center. Purl until 2 sts beyond the marker, p2tog, p1. Turn. Sl 1. Knit until 2 sts beyond the marker, sl 1, k1, psso, k1, and turn. *Sl 1. Purl until the last st before the "hole", p2tog, p1, and turn. Sl 1. Knit until the last st before the hole, sl 1, k1, psso, knit 1, and turn*; repeat between *s back and forth until there are no sts left on the outside of the hole. If you have used smaller needles for the purl rows on the heel, change to larger needles. Divide the 15 (15) 17 sts onto two needles. Using contrast color, pick up 9 (10) 10 sts in the "loops" on each side of the heel. If you don't have enough loops, pick up extra sts between needles 1 and 2, and 3 and 4. The sts from needles 2 and 3 are worked in the Main design. The sts on needles 1 and 4 are worked in the sole design, chosen from the small designs shown on separate charts. Start the design under the foot on needle 4. Work contrast color 1 st, main color 1 st, contrast color 1 st, then follow one the sole designs until 3 sts remain on needle 1, finishing off with contrast color 1 st, main color 1 st, and contrast color 1 st. Work the stripe design over the 3 sts on each side, the small design over remaining sts on needles 1 and 4, and the Main design over needles 2 and 3 until the toe shaping. Dec 1 st after the first 3

sts on needle 4, and before the last 3 sts on needle 1 every 4th rnd until 46 (50) 54 sts remain. Work until the foot measures 6¼" (6⅝") 7".

Shaping the toe: For the toe, use main color or contrast color only. Knit 1 rnd, knitting the last 2 sts on needle 1 together. Knit the first st on needle 2 using needle 1, and pass the k2tog st over from needle 1. Knit until the last 2 sts on needle 3, and repeat the dec. Dec 2 sts on each side every rnd until 10 sts remain. Put these sts on yarn and gather. Weave all loose ends into the back of the fabric. Steam lightly.

SKI STOCKINGS 1

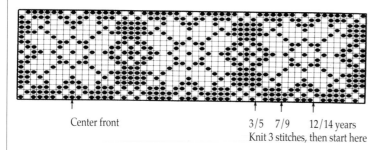

Center front   3/5   7/9   12/14 years
Knit 3 stitches, then start here

SKI STOCKINGS 2

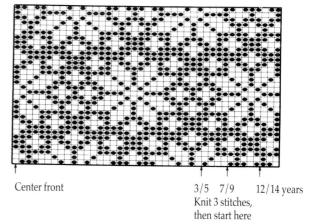

Center front   3/5   7/9   12/14 years
Knit 3 stitches,
then start here

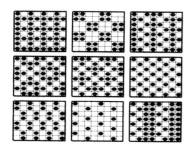

Small designs for the sole. Pick the one
you like best

SKI STOCKINGS 3

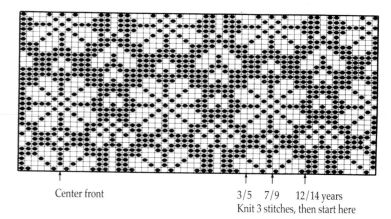

Center front   3/5   7/9   12/14 years
Knit 3 stitches, then start here

Turning Your Own Design into a Stocking

Make a design on graph paper. Make
sure you have enough repeats of the design
to cover a little more than half of the sts
needed. Mark the center of one repeat. Now
find the same center as far left as possible.
This is your center front st. Mark it. Subtract
4 sts from the number of sts required, and
divide this number by 2. Count the number
you get from the center st on your chart
going right. Put an arrow on the right side of
the last counted square. Start working the
design here after knitting the first 3 sts in
stripes (contrast, main, contrast color) on
needle 1. All the dec for the leg are done on
each side of these first 3 sts.

SKI STOCKINGS 4

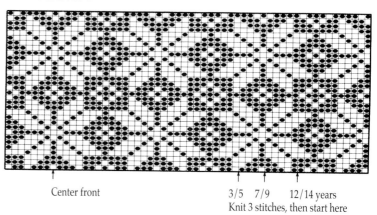

Center front   3/5   7/9   12/14 years
Knit 3 stitches, then start here

Socks

Basic Pattern for Leftover Yarns in Different Weights

We are convinced that homemade hand-knit socks are extra warm! How many of you have gotten a package from grandma containing socks? Your feet were warm for the longest time. Even if it's possible to buy wool socks for children, they're not quite the same. You need approximately 100g for a pair of socks, an excellent way of using up small scraps. On one account we disagree with grandma, though. Socks don't always have to be navy, grey, and olive colored, and absolutely not combined together! Because the socks require small amounts of yarn and are quick to make, they invite you to try some extra kicks on the aesthetic side. You'll probably have a lighter outlook on life on a rainy November day in if your socks are Rose with Gold borders rather than being dirty Green with Beige stripes. Use your imagination, and let your socks express some joy of life. Make solid-colored socks in a nice color, make stripes, or use a different color for the heel and toe. Duplicate stitch can do wonders to a pair of common ordinary socks. Stitch in a small motif, or the initials of the child to wear the socks. Small borders can also be decorative, either on the calf, or all over the sock. The simplest is to make the heel and the toe in solid color, and do a design over the rest of the sock, but there are no rules. Here are some basic patterns for socks, intended for scrap yarn of different weights. Usually socks are knit tighter than other garments to fit snugly, and to be more durable. For each pattern we'll give the regular needle size for the yarn, and the needle size for sock knitting to give you an impression of what scrap yarn fits each different sock pattern. If you knit tightly, it may be okay to use the regular needle size for socks. The socks will be extra durable if you knit the heel and toe using double strands. The extra strand could be the same yarn as the rest of the sock, if it is not too thick or too coarse. If so, the sock easily gets too bulky to wear. If the yarn you are using is bulky, use a finer yarn to double up for heels and toes. There are yarns specially made for socks, usually wool with some nylon. The problem with these yarns is the limited color choices. And you will not get rid of your scrap yarns if you buy new sock yarn. But you could use the sock yarn for the heels and toes only. You can add durability to the socks by knitting in a fine silk thread in a complimentary color. You may think of silk as only for fine, luxurious garments, rather than trivial winter socks. But silk fibers are very strong, and *at the same time*, silk is smooth and does not gnaw the wool fibers when the socks are in use. Wool and silk are actually somewhat related. Both are animal fibers, and both can be washed in lukewarm water and a mild wool detergent. There are yarns with a wool/silk blend. For heels and toes you can also knit thin silk embroidery thread together with wool yarn. It may sound extravagant, but you don't need much silk for a pair of socks for a child when you use it only for the heels and the toes.

Socks knit on sizes 2 and 3 (2.5mm and 3mm) needles

Sizes: 3/5 (7/9) 11/14 years
Yarn suggestion: Rauma Strikkegarn and
other yarns usually knit on needles sizes
3 and 4 (3mm and 3.5mm).
Amounts: Approximately 100g for all sizes.

Using smaller needles, cast on 40 (44) 48
sts. Join, being careful not to twist sts. Work
k2, p2 ribbing for 2¼" (2¾") 3⅛". Optional:
Make the ribbing twice as long to fold over.
A longer ribbing is practical if the socks are
used for boots. Change to larger needles and
work stockinette stitch for 1⅛" (1⅛") 1½".
This part can also be made longer.

Heel: Put the sts from needle 1 and needle
4 onto one needle—20 (22) 24 sts. Working
back and forth, the purl rows often come out
looser than the knit rows working back and
forth, so, working the heel, consider using
needles size 2 (2.5mm) for the purl rows, and
size 3 (3mm) for the knit rows. Work back
and forth for 1½" (2") 2¼". Slip the first st on
the row without knitting. The last row before
turning the heel should be a knit row.

Turning the heel: Mark the center 2 sts on
the needle. Purl until 2 sts beyond the 2
center sts, p2tog, p1, and turn. Knit until 2

sts beyond the 2 center sts, sl 1, k1, psso, k1,
and turn. *Slip the first st, purl until the st
before the "hole", p2tog (the st before and
after the hole), p1, and turn. Slip the first st,
knit until the st before the hole, sl 1, k1, psso,
k1, and turn*; repeat between *s across until
all the sts outside the hole are decreased.
Divide the sts from the heel onto 2 needles
again, and pick up 8 (9) 10 sts on each side of
the heel. Because you have slipped the first
st of each row, you'll have some "loops" on
each side of the heel. Pick up 1 st through
these loops, and 1 st between needle 1 and 2,
and between needle 3 and 4. Knit 1 rnd. You
now have more sts on needles 1 and 4 than
on needles 2 and 3. Dec 1 st at the end of
needle 1, and at the beginning of needle 4
every 4th rnd until 36 (42) 48 sts remain. The
decreases look good if done as follows: Knit
the 2 first sts on needle 4 together. At the end
of needle 1, sl 1, k1, psso. Work until the foot
measures approximately 4¾" (5½") 6¼",
including the heel.

Shaping the toe: Needle 1: *K1, k2tog. Knit
to the last 3 sts on the same needle, sl 1, k1,
psso, k1*; repeat between *s for the other 3
needles. Dec like this every 4th rnd 2 times,
then every other rnd until 8 sts remain. Put
remaining sts on yarn and gather. Weave all
loose ends into the back of the fabric.

Socks for babies and toddlers knit on sizes 2 and 3 (2.5mm and 3mm) needles

Sizes: 6 months (1 year) 2 years (3 years)
Yarn suggestion: Rauma Babygarn and
other yarns usually knit on needles sizes
2 and 3 (2.5mm and 3mm). For this pattern you are not using a smaller needle,
except if you knit loosely.
Amounts: Approximately 50g for the smallest sizes, maybe a little more for the
larger, depending on the yarn.

Using smaller needles, cast on 40 (44) 48
(48) sts. Join, being careful not to twist sts.
Work k1, p1 ribbing for 2" (2") 2¼" (2¾"),
decreasing 1 st on each needle for the 3
smallest sizes (no dec for the largest size).
Change to larger needles and knit 3 rnds.

Heel: Put the sts from needle 1 and needle
4 onto one needle—18 (20) 22 (24) sts on that
needle. Working back and forth, the purl
rows often come out looser than the knit
rows, so consider using one size smaller
needle for the purl rows in making the heel.
Work back and forth for 12 (14) 18 (22) rows.
Slip the first st on each row, and finish with a
knit row.

Turning the heel: Mark the 2 center sts on the needle. Purl until 2 sts beyond those 2 sts, p2tog, p1, turn. Slip the first st, knit until 2 sts beyond the 2 center sts, sl 1, k1, psso, k1, and turn. *Slip the first st and purl until the last st before the "hole". Purl the st before the hole together with the st after the hole, p1, and turn. Slip the first st off. Knit until the last st before the hole, sl 1, k1, psso, k1, and turn*; repeat between *s, working back and forth until all the sts outside the hole are decreased. Put the heel sts on two needles and pick up 7 (8) 10 (12) sts along each side of the heel. Because you have slipped the first st off every row, you have "loops" along each side. Pick the sts up in these loops, plus some extra between needles 1 and 2, and needles 3 and 4 if necessary. Using the larger needles only, dec 1 st at the end of needle 1, and at the beginning of needle 4 every other rnd until 36 (40) 44 (48) sts remain. Work until the foot measures 3⅛" (3¾") 4¼" (5⅛"), including the heel.

Shaping the toe: Knit the first st on needle 1, k2tog. Knit until 3 sts remain on the same needle, sl 1, k1, psso, k1. Repeat this procedure for the other 3 needles. Dec like this every 4th rnd 2 times, then every 2nd rnd until 8 sts remain. Put these sts on yarn, and gather. Weave all loose ends into the back of the fabric.

Socks for children knit on size 2 (2.5mm) needles

Sizes: 2 (4) 6 (8) 10 (12) years

Yarn suggestion: Rauma Gammel, Rauma Finullgarn, and other yarns usually knit on needles sizes 2 and 3 (2.5mm and 3mm). If you are using Rauma Finullgarn, the heel should be reinforced with silk, at least for older children. Finullgarn is loosely spun, and not intended for socks, but this yarn has been used for many models in this book, so you may have some left over. Finullgarn comes in many beautiful colors, and invites some fun sock knitting.

Amounts: Approximately 50g for the 3 smaller sizes, and closer to 100g for the 3 larger sizes.

Using smaller needles, cast on 40 (44) 48 (52) 56 (60) sts. Join, being careful not to twist sts. Work k1, p1 ribbing for 3/4" (1⅛") 1⅛" (1½") 1½" (1½"). Make sure you have the same number of sts on each needle. Knit in the rnd until the sock measures 2¼" (3⅛") 4" (4¾") 5½" (6¼").

Heel: Put the sts from needle 1 and needle 4 onto one needle—20 (22) 24 (26) 28 (30) sts on that needle. Work the heel over these sts, and knit in another strand of wool or silk for reinforcing. Slip the first st of each row, and work back and forth for 17 (19) 21 (23) 25 (27) rows, ending with a purl row.

Turning the heel: Mark the 2 center sts on the needle. Knit until 2 sts beyond the center sts, sl 1, k1, psso, k1, and turn. Slip the first st, purl until 2 sts beyond the center sts, p2tog, p1, and turn. *Sl 1, knit until the last st before the "hole", sl 1, k1, psso, k1, and turn. Sl 1, purl until the last st before the hole, p2tog, p1, and turn*; repeat between *s working back and forth until all the sts outside the hole are decreased. Put the heel sts back onto two needles, and work in the rnd dropping the reinforcing strand. *At the same time,* pick up 9 (10) 11 (12) 13 (14) sts on each side of the heel. Pick the sts up in the "loops" on each side, plus 1 st between needles 1 and 2, and needles 3 and 4. Divide the new sts equally on needles 1 and 4. On the first rnd, knit the new sts on each side of the heel through the back loop. Knit 3 rnds. Dec 1 st at the beginning of the 4th needle by knitting 2 together, and dec 1 st at the end of needle 1 by slipping 1, knitting 1, passing the slip stitch over. Repeat this dec every 3rd rnd until 40 (44) 48 (52) 56 (60) sts remain. Work even until the foot measures 3½" (4¼") 5⅛" (5⅞") 6⅝" (7½") from the pick up sts after finishing the heel.

Shaping the toe: Optional: Knit in a reinforcing strand for the toe. *Knit the 2nd and the 3rd st together on needle 1. Knit until 3 sts left on the same needle, k2tog, k1*; repeat this dec for the 3 other needles (8 dec on the rnd). Repeat the dec rnd every 3rd rnd 2 times, then every other rnd until 8 sts remain. Put these sts on yarn and gather. Weave all loose ends into the back of the fabric.

Socks for children using heavier yarn and sizes 3 and 4 (3mm and 3.5mm) needles

Sizes: 2–4 (6–8) 10–12 years

Yarn suggestion: Rauma Spælsaugarn, and other yarn usually knit on needles sizes 4 and 6 (3.5mm and 4mm). Rauma Spælsaugarn is a tightly spun 4-ply yarn, and is a good alternative to sock yarn with nylon.

Amounts: 50g for the smaller sizes, and 100g for the larger sizes.

Using smaller double-point needles, cast on 44 (48) 52 sts. Divide the sts equally on the four needles. Join, being careful not to twist sts. Work k1, p1 ribbing for 4¾" (5½") 6¼". Change to larger needles and knit 3 rnds.

Heel: Work the heel back and forth over the sts on needles 1 and 4. You may get a more even gauge using needle size 4 (3.5mm) on the knit rows, and needle size 3 (3mm) on the purl rows. Slip the first st of each row. Work back and forth for 1½" (2") 2¼", ending with a knit row.

Turning the heel: Mark the 2 center sts on the needle. Purl until 2 sts beyond the center sts, p2tog, p1, and turn. Sl 1, knit until 2 sts beyond the center sts, sl 1, k1, psso, k1, and turn. *Sl 1, purl until the last st before the "hole", p2tog, p1, and turn. Sl 1, knit until the last st before the hole, sl 1, k1, psso, k1, and turn*; repeat between *s until all the sts outside the hole are decreased. Put the heel sts back on two needles and pick up 8 (10) 12 sts on each side of the heel. Pick the sts up in the loops on each side. Knit 1 rnd. K2tog at the beginning of needle 4 and at the end of needle 1 every other rnd until 44 (48) 52 sts remain. Work until the foot measures 5⅛" (6⅝") 7⅞", including the heel.

Shaping the toe: Needle 1: Knit until 3 sts left on the needle, k2tog, k1. Needle 2: K1, k2tog, knit across. Needle 3: Knit until 3 sts left, k2tog, k1. Needle 4: K1, k2tog, knit across. Dec like this every other rnd 4 (5) 6 times, then every rnd until 8 sts remain. Put these sts on yarn and gather. Weave all loose ends into the back of the fabric.

Index

Sources

Charlotte's Web
137 Epping Road
Exeter, NH 03833
(603) 778-1417
Mail-order or retail sale of Rauma Finullgarn and Strikkegarn.

Nordic Fiber Arts
Four Cutts Road
Durham, NH 03824
(603) 868-1196
Mail-order or retail sale of all yarns used in this book.

Norsk Engros USA, Inc.
PO Box 229
Decorah, IA 52101
(800) 553-0014
Special order wholesale of Rauma Finullgarn and Istragarn.

The Unique
11 East Bijou St.
Colorado Springs, CO 80903
(719) 473-9406
Mail-order or retail sale of Rauma yarns.